W9-BUX-191

after the *Dreadful Conflagration* in the *Year* 1666.
— of the Fire; & the Perspective *that left Standing.*

References of remarkable places

A	Ludgate	V	Leaden Hall
B	Newgate	W	Dukes Palace
C	Aldersgate	X	Custom House
D	Cripplegate	Y	Bethlem
E	Moorgate	Z	Sion Colledge
F	Bishopsgate	a	Temples Stairs
G	Aldgate	b	White Fryers Stairs
H	Essex House	c	Black Fryers Stairs
I	The Temple	d	Puddle Dock
K	Dorset House	e	Pauls Wharf
L	Bridewell	f	Broken Wharf
M	Baynards Castle	g	Queen Hyth
N	Christ Church Cloyster	h	3 Cranes
O	S. Bartho. Hospital	i	Stilyard
P	Charter House	k	Coal Harbour
Q	Guild Hall	l	Old Swan
R	The Stokes	m	Billings gate
S	Royal Exchange	n	Tower Wharf
T	Gresham Colledge	o	Artillery Yard

THAMES

Part of Southwark

A Scale of half an English Mile.

10 20 30 40 50 Perches

WREN'S LONDON

1. *The Great Fire of London seen from Wapping.*

WREN'S LONDON

by Eric de Maré

THE FOLIO SOCIETY

London MCMLXXV

Wingate College Library

© Copyright The Folio Society Limited 1975

PRINTED IN GREAT BRITAIN
Printed and bound by Jarrold & Sons Ltd, Norwich
Set in 'Monophoto' Bembo 12 point spaced 1 point

082880

Contents

2. *The Choir of St Paul's Cathedral as rebuilt by Wren.*

Foreword

This work does not pretend to contain prime scholarship but it may possess some freshness in dealing for the first time, and in a comprehensive way, with the most dramatic decades in the long history of a great city. It describes the unhealthy, medieval warren of the Square Mile as it existed just before the Great Fire of 1666, the trauma of that Fire, how the inhabitants coped with the calamity and how they so urbanely rebuilt their city with the support of two outstanding men: a great monarch and a scientist of rare talents who, at a lucky moment, happened to be developing his flair as an amateur architect. It is a good old tale that can perhaps bear repetition in a new form.

I have stuck firmly to my last and have not considered Wren's works outside the City core, not even his great hospitals at Chelsea and Greenwich, nor his three churches outside the Wall: St Clement Danes in the Strand, St James's in Piccadilly, St Anne's in Soho. The information I have carpentered together has been culled from many sources, but mostly from a few standard works: Bell's *The Great Fire of London*, Reddaway's *The Rebuilding of London after the Great Fire*, Christopher Wren Junior's *Parentalia*, the *Diaries* of Pepys and Evelyn, Dutton's *The Age of Wren*, Cobb's *The Old Churches of London*, and the three monographs on Wren by Sir John Summerson, Margaret Whinney and Kerry Downes.

My thanks go to Andra Nelki for her invaluable help in finding the contemporary illustrations.

3. *Vischer's famous engraving of the City in 1616 seen from Southwark.*

1. Before the Fire

Shakespeare died in 1616, fifty years before the Great Fire, but even by 1666 the City of London had changed little since Tudor days; indeed it was still largely medieval in character just as Shakespeare had known it. Its appearance across the river, as revealed in Vischer's magnificent panorama completed the very year Shakespeare died, shows a romantic fairy-tale town with the variegated towers and spires of a hundred parish churches piercing the sky, and the river front a lively jumble of ships, warehouses, wharves and landing steps. The closely packed houses were mainly half-timbered with red-tiled roofs of the type still visible at Staples Inn, Holborn.

Seen from afar the City as a whole possessed an immutable coherence of scale and style where 'though all things differ all agree', and where, like any good composition however unpremeditated, it had its focal climax: the great Gothic cathedral of Old St Paul's rising on the western hill but now sadly lacking the soaring spire of timber and lead that had been struck by lightning and burned away in 1561. This was not England's finest fane and could not be compared in beauty with Salisbury, York or Lincoln, but it was dignified and grand, and among its attractions it possessed a lovely rose window.

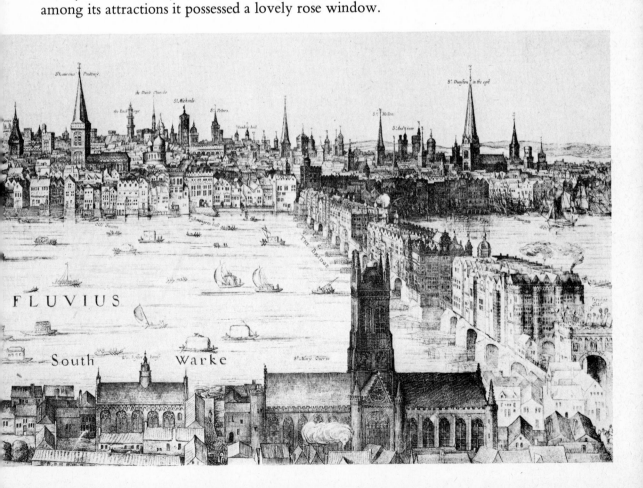

4. *Typical houses of pre-Fire London.*

The old bridge Peter Colechurch had completed back in 1209 after thirty-three years of effort is clearly delineated by Vischer. The substructure with its protective starlings projecting like long islands from each pier was still as Colechurch had designed it, but many changes had come to the houses it bore. London had no other bridge until 1750, when Labelye built a second at West-minster. Old London Bridge was, in fact, the City's greatest vested interest for it channelled all traffic into the City and there concentrated trade; thus when a new bridge between Westminster and Lambeth was proposed in 1664, the City Council sent delegates to Charles II to implore him to oppose the scheme, with the inducement of £100,000 – a bribe the king, being as usual 'plagued by a penury of pecune', readily accepted.

In 1616 the Bridge was at its grandest, not least on account of Nonsuch House which had replaced the Drawbridge Tower in 1577: there noblemen resided and it was, according to Stow, 'a beautiful and chargeable piece of work' built of timber framing, turreted and crowned with cupolas and golden weather vanes, well fenestrated with leaded panes to give wide views up and down the river. On Vischer's engraving can also be seen the southern Bridge Gate decorated on top with the heads of traitors stuck to the ends of long poles as a dire warning to plotters.

A closer view of the river front than Vischer's would have revealed a muddle of buildings and stinking laystalls where the City's night-soil and rubbish were dumped and where steep and narrow lanes, dangerous for the dray carts that used them, ran down to the river. Above them, the City itself, if still picturesque, was hardly romantic, as we shall see, but an insanitary, noisome, inconvenient and overcrowded slum.

In 1647 a panorama similar to Vischer's was engraved by the Bohemian artist Wenceslas Hollar whose fine depictions show London and Westminster both before and after the Fire. The shrivelling heads on their poles had gone; so also had some of the Tudor houses at the north end of the Bridge which were burned down in 1633 when a maidservant employed by a needle-maker carelessly left a pail of hot ashes under some stairs. These had now been replaced by

5. Hogenberg's map of Elizabethan London, published in 1572.

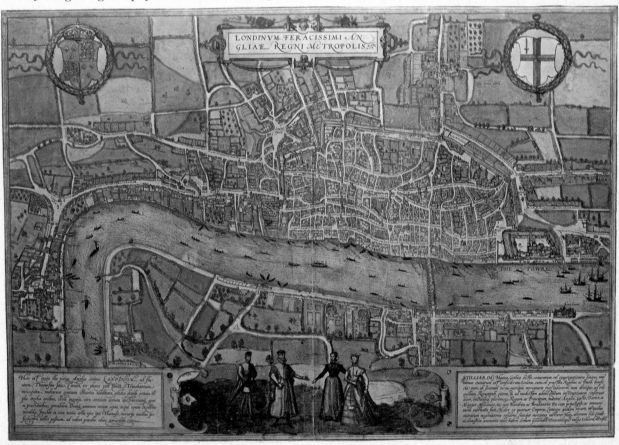

6. *Hollar's engraving of the Nave of Old St Paul's in 1658.*

regular three-storey blocks with dormered roofs and, according to a contemporary, 'stately platforms, leaded with rails and ballasters about them, very commodius and pleasant for walking and enjoying so fine a prospect up and down the river, and some had pretty little gardens with arbours'. Unfortunately these attractive terraces were to be destroyed by the Fire.

As a result of the austere years of the Commonwealth, the Globe Theatre, the bear gardens, the stews and other festive places on the south bank had disappeared, and since the start of the Civil War little had been built: architecture was in eclipse. Yet one important new building must be mentioned, even if it was not within the purlieus of the City but upstream at Westminster, centre of Law, Court and Government, which was linked to the City by a highway running through the village of Charing along the strand of the Thames where a row of fine palaces belonging to noblemen and prelates had gardens sloping down to the river. This new building, which set a precedent of immense importance to future developments in architectural style, not least in the works of Christopher Wren, was the famous Banqueting Hall by Inigo Jones, intended as the nucleus of a rebuilt royal palace. A design for this palace was put forward by John Webb,

Wingate College Library

the pupil and nephew of Inigo Jones, but, like a later one by Wren, it was never carried out.

Completed in 1622, and still in a perfect state today (having survived the fire that consumed the rambling Tudor palace of Henry VIII in 1698), the Banqueting Hall, with its single great room and its splendid ceiling painted by Rubens, was important in two ways: first as a royal symbol to glorify the House of Stuart, and secondly as an architectural innovation that must have startled Londoners with its sophisticated Palladian masonry, for its main façades containing rhythmical rows of tall windows, carved decorations and classical pilasters, all in mathematical, carefully proportioned precision, must have seemed to them more like a stage set than a building.

Inigo Jones, who became Surveyor to the Crown, was a great innovator, but little of his work has survived. The colonnade of houses, known as the Piazzas, which he laid out for the Earl of Bedford in Covent Garden, with the parish church of St Paul's at one end, was the important precursor of those domestic estates with frondy squares built for the aristocratic, land-owning speculators that form so unique and pleasant a part of inner London and belie the notion that London is a completely unplanned metropolis.

7. *A drawing of 1585 of the buildings and the church of St Michael in the Querne, at the west end of Cheapside, provides an impression of London before the Fire.*

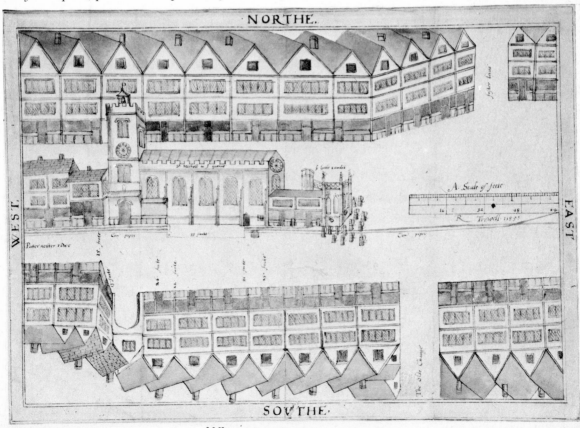

Wingate College Library

The growth of London built in the old haphazard ways outside the City Wall during the first half of the seventeenth century was prodigious. As John Evelyn wrote in 1648: 'To such a mad intemperance is the age come of building about a city by far too disproportionate already to the nation, I having in my time seen it almost as large again as it was within my memory.' At the start of the Stuart period, the population of the City, Westminster, the Liberties and the out-parishes was about a quarter of a million; by the year of the Great Fire it had risen to over four hundred thousand (in spite of the Great Plague which killed a hundred thousand and caused a large evacuation into the country); and by the end of the century, when the City had been almost completely rebuilt, it was touching seven hundred thousand. Trade, too, was continually on the increase, and by 1700 the tonnage of shipping that entered the Port of London was more than a third of the tonnage that arrived in the whole country.

8. *Covent Garden with its arcaded houses and parish church designed by Inigo Jones as the first of London's west-end squares.*

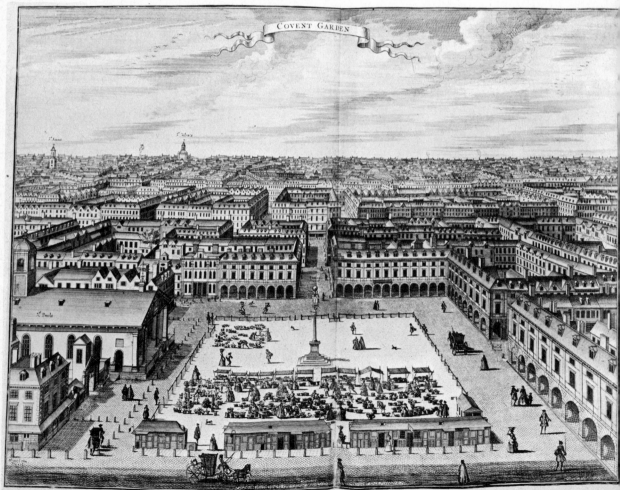

9. *A formalized painting of King James I and family listening to a sermon at St Paul's Cross outside the old Cathedral. Painted in 1616, the event itself did not take place until 1620.*

The Restoration year of 1660 was a jolly one, for the restrictive years of Puritan rule were over. The scene on 29 May has been preserved by John Evelyn. 'This day, after a sad and long exile, and after calamitous suffering of both the king and church for seventeen years, His Majesty King Charles II came to London: this day was also his birthday. He came with a triumph of over twenty thousand horse and foot brandishing their swords and shouting with unexpressable joy. The ways were strewn with flowers, the bells were ringing,

10. *Charles II's triumphal entry into the City at the Restoration in 1660.*

the streets were hung with tapestry, and the fountains were running wine. The mayor, aldermen and all the Companies, in their chains of gold, liveries and banners, were present; also the lords and nobles. Everybody was clad in cloth of silver, gold and velvet; the windows and balconies were all set with ladies, trumpets and music, and myriads of people flocked the streets as far as Rochester, so that they took seven hours to pass through the city – even from two in the afternoon till nine at night. I stood in the Strand and beheld it and blessed God.'

One of the many activities that the restored Charles II enjoyed was the new sport of yacht racing in beautiful little sailing craft all carved and gilded, and this sport, together with the Frost Fairs in cold winters and the Lord Mayor's Show (held on the river until the early nineteenth century when it took to the land) added to the gaiety of Restoration life. The Lord Mayor's Show of 1660 was particularly brilliant and, in *The Royal Cake*, John Tatham described how 'the barges, and all other companies, adorned with streamers and banners, and fitted with hautboys, cornets, drums and trumpets, being in the water, move towards Westminster, and by the way his lordship is saluted with twenty pieces of ordnance, as peals of entertainment and joy'.

The Royalists who returned at the Restoration tended by choice to settle outside the City in more open and pleasanter areas to the west, particularly if they were courtiers despising the traders of the merchant city. Pepys was one of the few men of affairs who still lived in the City, and from his immortal diary the place comes restlessly alive. He visits a banker in Lombard Street, rolls through the Shambles where his coach knocks some joints of meat into the mire that costs him a shilling in pacification, sits in a church listening critically to a sermon, goes to the theatre in Fleet Street, to the shops with two ladies to buy a petticoat, to a tavern for a pint of ale, to a chop house for a meal, to a respectable brothel for other needs, to the stairs by the Bridge to take a wherry up river to Westminster on business or to Vauxhall Gardens on pleasure. Of the actual fabric of London, however, Pepys gives us no clear verbal picture, and for that we must turn to contemporary prints.

The City Wall had long since decayed along the riverside, but a view from the tower of, say, Gresham's Royal Exchange would have revealed that, some two miles long, it was still intact elsewhere, pierced here and there by various Gates. Outside the Wall, London was spreading both east and west so that the tripartite division of City core, East End and West End was already evident.

A closer view of the City than the grand and distant panoramas of Vischer and Hollar would have brought a rude awakening to realities. Most of it was composed of dark, tortuous streets and alleys, and of timber-framed houses closely packed. These houses were two or three storeys high, and above them rose the bell-towers of the numerous parish churches – a contrast in scale with our own day when the churches are drowned by the dreary, faceless towers of monopolistic modern commerce and when even St Paul's is struggling to preserve its identity amidst the ill-mannered indignities of impersonal and uncivilized power.

Here and there an open space would bring relief to a wanderer within the Wall: a churchyard, a wide market place or the garden of some grand dwelling of a wealthy merchant such as Crosby Hall (now rebuilt at Chelsea). Apart from such rarities and the old cathedral and the larger churches, the other important buildings were the Halls of the City Companies, some of them acquired as spoils from the monasteries after the Dissolution. Indeed, along the main streets stood many a grand monastic structure now debased to some lay purpose: the old cloistered monastery of Grey Friars in Newgate Street, for example, remained

intact until the Fire destroyed it, becoming a school for poor children known as
Christ's Hospital, while the chancel of its church was used for parochial worship
and its nave as a warehouse where the Stationers stored their books; the Pinners
Company acquired the refectory of Austin Friars as its Hall. In 1666 the ecclesiastical spirit of medieval England was therefore still much in evidence and not
until rebuilt after the Fire did the City assume that purely commercial aspect it
still retains.

Foreigners who had seen the splendours of the Italian towns were not
impressed by the City. No planning authority existed, nor did any tradition of
civic pride in the environment; citizens in general were either excessively
individualistic or purely parochial in their outlook, and town planning and
organization, even on a local basis, was nobody's business. Legislation was of an
entirely negative and restrictive nature. Medieval towns were rarely deliberately
planned with an eye for organized effect; they were *ad hoc* and utilitarian.

11. *Inigo Jones, masque
designer and inaugurating
architect.*

12. *The gorgeous annual procession when the Lord Mayor, Councillors and Companies proceeded up river in their carved and gilded barges to Westminster to pay their respects to the monarch.*

Restoration London, even after the Plague had reduced the population, was more crowded than it had ever been. Trade in all the necessities and luxuries of the world was flourishing, and along Thames Street the warehouses and cellars were bursting with commodities. But the City was not only a great mart and port; it was also a centre of considerable manufacture, as the existence of the wealthy Companies and Guilds gave evidence. The dirt came not only from refuse but also from the burning of sea-coal from Newcastle in domestic hearths as well as in the furnaces of soap-boilers, dyers, brewers and other manufacturers. Fogs were indeed as frequent in Restoration London as they were to be in Victorian London. They so distressed John Evelyn that, in his indignation, he wrote his *Fumifugium; or the Inconvenience of the Air and Smoke of London Dissipated.* It is this horrid smoke, Evelyn wrote, 'which obscures our churches and makes our palaces look old, which fouls our clothes and corrupts the waters, so that the very rain and refreshing dews which fall in the several seasons precipitate this impure vapour, which with its black and tenacious quality spots and contaminates whatever is exposed to it.' London's impure mists and filthy vapours, Evelyn pointed out, caused among the inhabitants of this one city more than in the whole earth besides the raging 'of vile catarrhs, phthisics, coughs and consumptions'. Yet the authorities did not discourage the burning of coal because large taxes could be raised from its import into London. The king, however, warmly commended Evelyn's proposals to mitigate the nuisance and commanded him to prepare a Bill on the matter for presentation to parliament. Five years later the whole City went up in horrid smoke.

The use of brick in the City had been encouraged for a long time, partly to reduce the number of fires but partly also to save timber which was in short supply owing to over-felling and was badly needed for building ships. Although London had had its Building Acts since those promulgated by its first Lord Mayor in 1189 whereby party walls were to be of stone or brick to stop fire spreading, they were rarely observed. Foundations might be of brick or stone, but walls were of timber, lath and plaster. On street fronts the upper storeys often projected in order to give weather protection below, sometimes so much so that the inhabitants could lean out and shake hands from opposite windows. Many alleys, therefore, were often dark even in daytime.

Streets and market places were paved with cobblestones set in gravel down the middle of which ran gutters where waste water and refuse were thrown, refuse being collected from time to time by scavengers for deposit in one of the many laystalls on the outskirts of the City or along the river front. No raised pavements protected the pedestrian from passing traffic and few bollasters existed. Rain dripped straight from the eaves into the streets, for gutters and down-pipes were rare, a fact lamented by Evelyn as 'the troublesome and malicious disposal of the spouts and gutters overhead', which rendered the labyrinth of passages 'a continual wet day after the storm is over'. Sewage went either into streams like the Fleet or into cesspits below the houses, and no public lavatories existed: even Mrs Pepys had on one recorded occasion to stoop in public and 'there in a corner do her business'.

13. *Londoners flee from the Plague.*

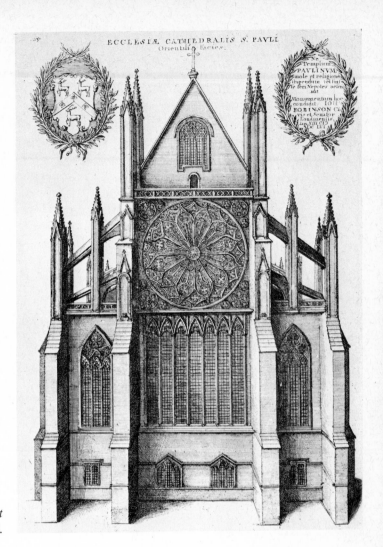

14. *Hollar's engraving of the east elevation of Old St Paul's in 1658.*

The wealthier merchants lived around Throgmorton Street, the Royal Exchange and Tower Street, with their counting houses at street level, apartments above and perhaps warehouses behind. Lesser breeds like shopkeepers traded from the ground floors of their homes, and there craftsmen had their workshops with living accommodation above for families and apprentices. In the wider streets the stalls and baskets of hawkers clustered thickly, while barrows, carriages, carts and sedan chairs added to the din and confusion. The dead were packed into the churchyards and the poor in great numbers into dark, squalid tenements, entire families being crammed into single rooms, often in the cellars. The overcrowding was as appalling as it was to become when London exploded in Victorian times.

The medieval thoroughfares of the old City had been built to take pedestrians and pack-horses only; during the seventeenth century the considerable growth

15. *Another Hollar engraving of Old St Paul's in 1658. It includes the steeple which, in fact, had burned down in 1561.*

of the wheeled traffic so essential to the City's life made them totally inadequate. Year by year the traffic jams grew worse and pedestrians were driven to the walls.

Some three thousand watermen rowing for hire on the river were growing ever more anxious about their livelihoods with the increase of the Hackney Hell Carts and the new sedan chairs that had arrived in London in 1634. John Taylor, the Water Poet who became royal waterman and was the self-appointed Public Relations Officer of his kind, called attention to the plight of his fellows in a 'rattling, rowling and rumbling age'. He broke into a song of protest:

> *Carroaches, coaches, jades and Flanders mares*
> *Do rob us of our shares, our wares, our fares;*
> *Against the ground we stand and knock our heels,*
> *Whilst all our profit runs away on wheels.*

In fact the wheeled traffic did not greatly affect the watermen for citizens continued to use their river as a main, wide, airy high street which provided the most pleasant, safe and rapid means of conveyance from one side of the City to the other. With the increase of population and business, wherries as well as carriages were in demand. The river also supplied a good deal of domestic water with the help of the pumping wheels, worked by the tides, that the Dutchman, Pieter Morice, had installed beneath the northern arch of the Bridge in 1580. Water supplies were, if not too clean, at least adequate as a result not only of the Bridge wheels but also of various springs and wells and of the channel of the New River Company.

One aggravation of the street congestion was the placing of water conduits at street crossings. Another was the blockage caused by the street markets. A third, and major one, was that of purprestures – the foolish official permits to extend buildings into the streets. Charles II tried to reduce the most serious bottlenecks by an Act of 1662, but nothing was really accomplished until the Fire ruthlessly enforced a solution to the whole problem of street improvement.

The City, in fact, provided the perfect seed bed both for plague and conflagration. Pestilence, endemic since the early Middle Ages, in some years became pandemic, and in Tudor days if deaths from plague exceeded fifty a week, all the theatres were closed to prevent its spread. Between 1094 and the Great Plague of 1665 London suffered twelve serious outbreaks. Dysentery, typhus, smallpox and the sweating sickness or *Sudor Anglicus* (mortal in three hours) were always prevalent, but the mass killer was Bubonic Plague. In 1603, in London, some thirty thousand died from it, and even more in 1625;

16. *This painting of the Coronation Procession of Edward VI conveys a general, if formalized, impression of the City before the Fire.*

there was a further minor outbreak in 1636 and then came the Great Plague, a return of the Black Death which had ravaged Europe three centuries before.

With its pocket full of posies and its atishoo, atishoo, Bubonic Plague was carried by rats brought to London in ships; fleas sucked their blood and deposited the microbes in the bodies of human beings. Floor rushes, wall hangings, and dirty clothes and bedding harboured the fleas while the rats found comfortable quarters everywhere in the hollow walls of the houses. The outbreak began early in the summer of 1665 in the suburb of St Giles's-in-the-Fields, and soon the death toll was mounting rapidly until, as a contemporary recorded, 'there is a dismal solitude in London streets. Now shops are shut in, people rare, and very few that walk about, insomuch as the grass begins to spring up in some places and a deep silence in every place, especially within the walls . . . The nights are too short to bury the dead; the long summer days are spent from morning until twilight in conveying the vast number of dead bodies into the bed in their graves.'

Pepys had bravely stayed in London to carry on his navy job, and as late as 20 September he wrote: 'But Lord, what a sad time it is, to see no boats upon the river – and grass grow up and down Whitehall-court – and nobody but poor wretches in the streets.'

As well as providing comfortable quarters for rats, the hollow walls of the houses also, like chimneys, encouraged flames with rising draughts, and it was only after the Fire, when brick and stone replaced timber, when floors were boarded, tiled or carpeted, and when the brown rats (which carried fewer fleas than the black ones) began killing off their darker peers with that racial discrimination of which Nature is brutally fond, that the main causes of plague and fire were at last eliminated. So, in spite of the upheaval and dispossession it imposed, the Great Fire proved in the end to be a great mercy.

2. *Doctor Wren*

An only son, Christopher Wren was born of patrician stock, in 1632, in the village of East Knoyle in Wiltshire where his father was then Rector, though soon to be appointed, in place of his brother Matthew, Dean of Windsor. It was the year that Galileo published his famous *Dialogo*. The Civil War began when Christopher was ten and until the Restoration his family suffered troubles. His uncle Matthew, now Lord Bishop of Ely, was imprisoned in the Tower for eighteen years for his royalist sympathies and his High Church views, while the Deanery at Windsor was twice raided so that his father was forced to seek refuge elsewhere.

Yet, in spite of the hard times, Christopher received a good education and of this he made the most – first from a tutor, then for a time at Westminster School, and finally at Wadham College, Oxford. In his early teens he wrote on many subjects in both English and Latin and he was full of invention, producing among other things a pneumatic engine, a device for writing in the dark, a model of the solar system, and another of the motion of the moon. Having taken his M.A. in 1653 he worked at research for four years at All Souls College, Oxford, and in 1657 was chosen as Professor of Astronomy at Gresham College in Bishopsgate, London. He returned to Oxford in 1661 as Savilian Professor of Astronomy. Not until he was nearly thirty years old when, as a don, he had reached the top of the academic tree, did he begin to take a serious interest in architecture.

Wren moved in the intellectual circle of Experimental Philosophers, scientists (though not yet called so) of encyclopaedic interests in the tradition of Aristotle, who sought universal truths in an age before atomized and myopic specialization had become necessary. A scholar might then be knowledgeable in Latin, physics, chemistry, optics, mechanics, astronomy and medicine, and be at the same time concerned with the improvement of industries, town planning, and the art and science of building. The educated man was the universal man, *Homo universalis*, of the type that cannot be bred today, though he was, in fact, the progenitor of the Industrial Revolution and the modern world.

Christopher Wren, a supreme example of the universal man, was one of the first to join the new and gentlemanly profession of architecture that replaced the guiding craftsmanship of the Master Mason and Master Carpenter of the Middle Ages. Such men had of necessity to be largely self-taught since they had few professional precedents to guide them and no schools of architecture or system of apprenticeship to instruct them. In Wren's case a taste for drawing, at which he was adept, together with a love of making models from the results of his researches, stimulated his desire to design buildings.

At the close of the Civil War a group of intelligent men of insatiable curiosity, creative energy and adventurous zest had formed a club 'for the promotion of Physico–Mathematical Experimental learning' which, in 1660, under the king's patronage and charter, was renamed the Royal Society. Wren naturally became a member of the Society together with such as Robert Boyle, Robert Hooke, Samuel Pepys, John Evelyn and John Aubrey of *Brief Lives* fame.

Newton called Wren one of the three greatest geometers of his age, and having a reputation as such he may have been consulted early in life on structural problems. His first major architectural work was the Sheldonian Theatre in Oxford, a large hall in the form on plan of a Roman theatre where university ceremonies could be held; its foundation stone was laid in 1664. As the first effort of an amateur it is a remarkable *tour de force* particularly in its solution of the problem of roofing a wide space with timbers. At about the same time he designed the chapel for Pembroke College, Cambridge, a surprisingly mature work which was completed in 1665 as a gift from his uncle, Bishop Matthew Wren.

Wren's family had Court connections and in 1661, when he had returned to Oxford as Professor of Astronomy, Christopher was noticed by Charles II to whom he had presented some drawings of animacules seen through a

17. *Hollar's engraving of the old Royal Exchange that was burned in the Fire.*

Hanc Tabulam invenit & incepit Anton: Verrio, Perfecerunt Gothofredus Kneller & Joc: Thornhill Equites.

18. *Sir Christopher Wren and the rebuilt City. He holds the plan of St Paul's in his hand.*

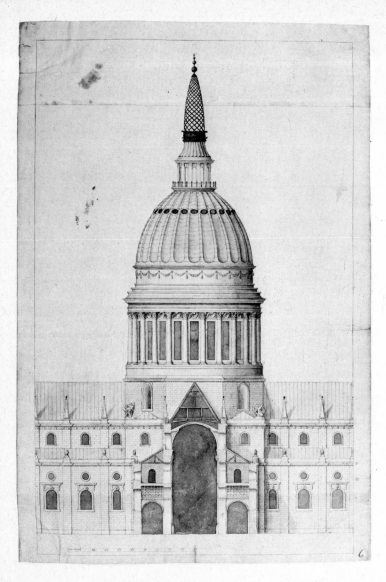

19. *Wren's drawing for reconstructing Old St Paul's Cathedral, including a splendid new Renaissance drum and a dome topped by a pine-cone.*

microscope and also a model of the moon. The loyalty to the Crown of the Wren family was no doubt a strong recommendation, although it is clear that the astute monarch had early recognized the exceptional gifts and potentialities of the young man whom Evelyn had lauded as 'that miracle of a youth' when he was twenty-one and ten years later as 'that incomparable genius'. Evelyn, who had the royal ear, no doubt commended him to the king. The king invited Wren to go to Tangier (now under British rule as part of the dowry brought to Charles by his queen, Catherine of Braganza) to organize the harbour works and fortifications there, promising him as inducement the post of Surveyor of Works on the death or retirement of Sir John Denham. Wren declined the invitation on grounds of health, possibly a valid excuse because, although he lived to the age of ninety-one, he had been a delicate child.

A visit to France in the Plague year, his first and only venture abroad, had an important influence not only on the design he was to submit for the renewal of Old St Paul's, but on much of his later work, including the great new cathedral he was to build after the Fire.

Much of Wren's life has been recorded in a curious scrapbook compilation by his son (also named Christopher), published by his grandson Stephen in 1750 under the title *Parentalia or Memoirs of the Family of the Wrens; viz of Matthew Bishop of Ely, Christopher Dean of Windsor etc. but chiefly of Sir Christopher Wren*. It records that 'In the Year 1665, Mr Wren took a journey to Paris where, at that time all arts flourished in a higher degree than had ever been known before in France; and where was a general congress of the most celebrated masters in every profession, encouraged by royal munificence and the influence of the great Cardinal Mazarin. How he spent his time in that place will in

20. *Wren's sectional drawing of his projected drum and double dome for Old St Paul's.*

21. *Wright's portrait of Charles II.*

part appear from a short account he gave by letter to a particular friend . . . "I have", says he, "busied myself in surveying the most esteemed fabrics of Paris, and the country round; the Louvre for a while was my daily object, where no less than a thousand hands are constantly employed in the works . . . Bernini's design of the Louvre I would have given my skin for, but the old reserved Italian gave me but a few minutes view . . . I had only time to copy it in my fancy and memory."'

Wren was particularly thrilled by the great new baroque domes in Paris of Mansart and Lemercier's Church of the Val-de-Grâce and the latter's Church of the Sorbonne, then near completion. He inspected other domes too, such as the small one of Mansart's Church of the Visitation and probably the complex one of the Church of Sainte Anne-la-Royale by the Italian Guarini (long since vanished). All such domes were the children of the huge prototype of St Peter's in Rome.

Wren visited many other buildings in and around Paris, including the big houses and royal palaces. Wherever he could he watched work in progress noting the 'engines' used and the building techniques and organization. He was

22. *Wren's Coat of Arms.*

23. *Young Christopher Wren, son of the architect. He compiled* Parentalia, *the family history.*

particularly impressed by the quays along the Seine, and these no doubt he later had in mind when planning the riverside and the Fleet Canal in post-Fire London. He learned a great deal on this visit to France but he also had other sources of self-instruction. At home he could study the inaugural buildings of Inigo Jones, whom he admired, as well as those of John Webb. He could also study books, prints, drawings and paintings, Italian, Dutch and Flemish. He had read the works of Vitruvius in Latin as a youth, he read Sir Henry Wotton's *Elements of Architecture* of 1624, with its many Italian Renaissance ideas and he came to possess an excellent reference library to stimulate both mind and eye.

Wren returned to England in the spring of 1666 and began at once to prepare a report for the Royal Commission that had been formed in 1663 to deal with the reconstitution of Old St Paul's, the fourth cathedral on the site. The first had been demolished under the persecutions of Diocletian, but under Constantine it had been rebuilt, probably on the old foundations. The pagan Saxons destroyed this second edifice but the church was again restored in the seventh century. In 1083 this was burned down, and a fourth fane in Romanesque style arose which was added to at different times, both east and west. Old St Paul's was therefore partly round-arched Norman and partly pointed Gothic with a Latin cross plan. Inigo Jones had refaced the outside of the nave, replacing buttresses with classical pilasters, and he had built a fine, if incongruous, Corinthian portico at the west end in Portland stone, as can be seen in Hollar's engravings.

The cathedral had been in a poor condition for some time for it had been profaned by Cromwell's soldiers, who had used it as a cavalry barracks. Jones's portico had been defaced and used for shops, some displaying lewd prints. The squalid interior had served as a rendezvous for lawyers and their clients, as an employment exchange, as a market, and as a promenade for doxies. Much repair was needed.

Wren's report, presented in May 1666, was embellished by exquisite pen drawings in pale brown ink that revealed his skill as an architectural draughtsman. He had enjoyed himself and said that, even were his designs to prove unacceptable, 'I shall not repent the great satisfaction and pleasure I have taken in the contrivance which equals that of poetry or compositions in music'.

His proposals were fairly drastic. The crossing would be enlarged and covered with a double-skinned dome eighty feet in diameter and carried on four huge piers supporting arches and rising from a high rotondo. The upper dome was to be encircled by a gallery and would carry a wooden lantern topped by a curious pine-cone making a total height of three hundred and sixty feet, a height nearly equal to that of the existing cathedral. The nave was to be encased with new stonework with a giant Corinthian order. The old tottering tower was to be used ingeniously as scaffolding during construction of the dome and then demolished. From the sectional drawing of the scheme can be seen the effect of his Paris visit, and also the precedent for the dome of his great cathedral, today so familiar a City landmark.

Against much opposition Wren's proposals were finally accepted on 27 August. Six days later the Great Fire broke out, and Old St Paul's emerged as an unstable, calcined ruin. A new and dramatic situation arose that was to prove fateful for the whole future of the City, the cathedral and Wren's career as an architect.

3. Holocaust

Before the event the seers delivered dire prophecies in sonorous Biblical phrases. Thus Walter Gasteloin in 1658: 'London, go on still in thy presumptuous wickedness! Put the evil day far from thee, and repent not! Do so London. But if fire makes not ashes of the city, and thy bones also, conclude me a liar for ever. Oh, London! London! sinful as Sodom and Gomorrah! the decree has gone out, Repent, or burn, as Sodom, as Gomorrah!'

In his *Vision which he saw concerning London*, published in 1660, the persecuted Quaker, Humphrey Smith, produced an astonishing prediction: 'And as for the city, herself and her suburbs, and all that belonged to her, a fire was kindled therein; but she knew not how, even in all her goodly places, and the kindling of it was in the foundation of all her buildings, and there was none could quench it. And the burning thereof was exceedingly great, and it burned inward in a hidden manner which cannot be described . . . and it consumed all the lofty things therein, and the fire searched out all the hidden places, and burned most of the street places . . . neither did the burning hurt them, but they walked as dejected, mournful people . . . And the fire continued, for, though all the lofty part was brought down, yet there was much old stuffe, and parts of broken-down desolate walls, which the fire continued burning against. And the vision thereof remained in me as a thing that was showed me of the Lord.'

As many will know, the fire started among a pile of faggots beside the oven

24. *The Fire of London Medal.*

25. *Samuel Pepys in 1666 at the age of thirty-three.*

on the premises of one Farynor, king's baker, in Pudding Lane near London Bridge at about one-thirty of the morning of Sunday, 2 September 1666. In Evelyn's memorable words, 'This fatal night, at about ten, began that deplorable fire near Fish Street in London'. (The diarist was never very accurate about time.) The summer had been long and dry, and Pudding Lane was a dark, narrow street of pitch-covered timber houses running steeply down to Thames Street and dimly lit at night by candles shining here and there through windows of translucent horn. The seat of the fire was therefore a place where flames would spread rapidly. Farynor afterwards declared his conviction that it had

LEX IGNEA:
OR
The School of Righteousness.

A
SERMON

Preach'd before the KING,
Octob. 10. 1666.
At the SOLEMN FAST appointed
For the late
FIRE in LONDON.

By *WILLIAM SANDCROFT*, D. D.
Dean of S. *Pauls.*

Published by His Majestie's Special Command.

Etiam periere Ruinæ

London, Printed for R. *Pawlett*, at the Bible in *Chancery-lane* near *Fleetstreet.*

26. *Title page of the sermon preached before the king by the Dean of St Paul's after the Fire with its dramatic engraving of the old Cathedral in full blaze.*

been deliberately started by someone of evil intent, since his oven had long since been drawn. He with his wife, daughter and man, aroused by the smoke, escaped over the roofs, but his maidservant, not daring the climb, perished in the flames as first of the Fire's few victims.

At three o'clock in the morning the Pepys's household in Seething Lane, near the Tower, were roused by their maid Jane, who told them of the fire she had spotted away to the west. Pepys slipped on his nightgown to peer through her window across the roof tops, but he was unimpressed and went back to bed. From his house in Gracechurch Street the Lord Mayor also looked out and declared, 'Pish! a woman might piss it out'. Fires, after all, were no novelty in the City.

Soon the Star Inn near the bakery was blazing, but the trouble really began when the flames reached Thames Street and its warehouses full of combustibles such as oil, spirits, tallow, resin and hemp behind wharves piled with hay, coal and timber. Next, the nave and tower of St Magnus the Martyr by the bridgehead were alight and then the new terrace houses on the Bridge itself. Happily a break in the housing of the bridge, not filled since the conflagration there in 1632, prevented any further damage, though, less happily, the debris from the houses fell into the roadway blocking passage from the south so that no help in fighting the flames could arrive from Bankside.

The houses at the north end of the bridge were blazing away at eight o'clock when Pepys was up and about. He looked out and, since daylight had reduced the visual drama, he thought the fire was under control. 'By and by Jane comes

27. *Engines such as these could hardly have prevented the spread of the Great Fire.*

and tells me that she hears that above three-hundred houses have been burned down tonight by the fire we saw, and that it is now burning down all Fish Street by London Bridge. So I made myself ready presently, and walked to the Tower and there got up upon one of the high places, Sir J. Robinson's little son going up with me; and there I did see the houses at that end of the bridge all on fire, and an infinite great fire on this and the other side the end of the bridge – which, among other people, did trouble me for poor little Michell and our Sarah on the Bridge. So down, with my heart full of trouble, to the Lieutenant of the Tower, who tells me that it begun this morning in the king's baker's house in Pudding-lane, and that it hath burned down St Magnus's Church and most part of Fish Street already. So I down to the water-side and there got a boat and through bridge, and there saw a lamentable fire. Poor Michell's house, as far as the Old Swan, already burned that way and the fire running further . . .'

The day was cloudless and sunny but a fresh wind was blowing from the north-east to help spread the flames. Before long Fishmongers' Hall was alight, the first of the forty-four Halls of the City Companies to perish. The water house by the Bridge connected with Morice's waterwheels beneath the northern arches soon followed, so that the water system with its pumps could no longer be used to stay the fire, which now began to spread along the riverside towards the west and then, more slowly, up into the heart of the City.

Early in the day the Lord Mayor was advised to pull down or blow up houses to stop the progress of the fire, but he hesitated, asking how he could do so without the consent of the owners, and who would pay for their rebuilding. By noon of the first day, however, attempts were being made to pull down some houses in the path of the flames, but being too close to them, the effort proved futile. The fire was already out of hand and some church bells began pealing backwards to spread the alarm.

Yet in most of the City the Sunday routine continued as usual; the parish churches were filled and there was as yet little panic. At Whitehall the king and Court were unmoved until Pepys arrived at eleven o'clock and gave an account that dismayed them all. The king commanded Pepys to return at once to the City to instruct the Lord Mayor to pull down the houses in front of the flames everywhere. Now the clouds of smoke against the cloudless blue sky began to alarm the whole population. Wars with the Dutch and French were being waged and rumours of reprisals against the English incendiarism at Brandaris ran around the city. A papist plot was suspected and caused one man to gallop down Fleet Street shouting, 'Arm, arm!'

A Dr Taswell, then a boy at Westminster School, later recalled how 'the ignorant and deluded mob . . . vented forth their rage against the Roman Catholics and Frenchmen; imagining these incendiaries (as they thought)

28. *An old painting of the Great Fire seen from Ludgate.*

had thrown red-hot balls into the houses. A blacksmith in my presence, meeting an innocent Frenchman walking along the street, felled him instantly to the ground with an iron bar . . . In another place I saw the incensed populace divesting a French painter of all the goods he had in his shop; and, after having helped him off with many other things, levelling his house to the ground.'

Panic now began to bite and in the next three days pandemonium reigned. The high wind carried live sparks aloft which descended everywhere on the dry buildings. The wind, rising to a bellowing gale, fanned the flames, and spread the fire rapidly. An ancient custom in old London had been to place buckets of water, ladders, axes and fire-hooks at the end of long poles for pulling down walls and rafters at every church and at some of the Companies' Halls, but the custom had become neglected owing to the improved water supplies. Thus fire-fighting apparatus was nowhere conveniently at hand so that many fled in despair from their homes with as many of their possessions as they could carry or trundle, hundreds of them down to the riverside to hire a wherry that would carry them away from the horror. Soon the watermen were escalating their fares and making such profits that they made no attempts to save their own Hall and its contents.

Pepys too was concerned for his bags of gold, his chattels and his wine. But he had time to observe, and later to record, the growing confusion: 'Everybody endeavouring to remove their goods, and flinging into the river or bringing them into lighters that lay off. Poor people staying in their houses so long as till the very fire touched them, and then running into boats or clambering from one pair of stairs by the waterside to another . . . Having stayed, and in an hour's time seen the fire rage every way, and nobody to my sight endeavouring to quench it, but to remove their goods and leave all to the fire; and having seen it get as far as the Steelyard, and the wind mighty high and driving it into the City, and everything, after so long a drought, proving combustible, even the very stones of the churches . . .'

29. *John Evelyn, civil servant and diarist.*

Walking along Watling Street, as well as he could, Pepys saw 'every creature coming away loaden with goods to save – and here and there sick people carried away in beds'. The streets were 'full of nothing but people and horses and carts loaden with goods, ready to run over one another, and removing goods from one burned house to another'. Pigeons fluttered about the roofs and balconies until their wings were singed and they fell to the ground.

The fire began to spread uphill into the centre of the City and the general alarm was increased when the spire of St Laurence Poultney with its new peal of bells took fire and was visible from every quarter. The Trained Bands were hastily assembled to watch out for foreign incendiarists, and the king sent in his Guards. The Lord Mayor (Sir Thomas Bludworth, a vintner whose daughter married Judge Jeffreys) lost his head; a contemporary recorded that in Cannon Street 'we met my Lord Mayor on horseback, with a few attendants, looking like one frightened out of his wits'. The comment of Pepys, who disliked the man, was no less scathing: 'At last met my Lord Mayor in Canning Street, like a man spent, with a handkercher about his neck. To the king's message, he cried like a fainting woman, "Lord, what can I do? I am spent. People will not obey me. I have been pull[ing] down houses. But the fire overtakes us faster than we can do it".'

On the Sunday afternoon the king and his brother the Duke of York travelled down river from Whitehall in the royal barge and were joined by Pepys. The king was stirred by what he saw and gave vigorous and speedy instructions for the pulling down of more houses, sometimes approaching the flames so close that he was himself in peril. But little official action was organized that day; the sudden and rapidly growing catastrophe seemed to stupefy everyone.

When night fell the full, glaring horror of the spreading conflagration became dramatically evident. Pepys repaired to an alehouse on Bankside with his wife and a few friends and 'there stayed till it was dark almost and saw the fire grow; and as it grew darker, appeared more and more, and in corners and upon steeples and between churches and houses, as far as we could see up the hill of the City, in a most horrid malicious bloody flame, not like the fine flame of an ordinary fire . . . We stayed till, it being darkish, we saw the fire as only one entire arch of fire from this to the other side of the bridge, and in a bow up the hill, for an arch of above a mile long. It made me weep to see it. The churches, houses, and all on fire and flaming at once, and a horrid noise the flames made, and the cracking of houses at their ruin. So home with a sad heart . . .'

Barges and wherries crossed the river all that night through the glaring reflections on the rippling water, heaped with refugees and their household goods or traders with their merchandise, and often sharply silhouetted against the white stonework of the old bridge. No one had ever seen a fire like this before.

Monday was another sunny day and the wind continued to blow. As the fire spread posts were set up at some distance from the flames composed of soldiers and civilian volunteers, each with its provision of bread, cheese and ale, the aim being to form wide fire-breaks by demolitions; eventually seamen were summoned from the dockyards, being adept in handling ropes, chains and gunpowder. The fire now spread, not only up the hill but along the riverside to the west so that Baynard's Castle on the south-west corner of the City was soon afire. In the City that Monday night the Post Office was burned down with all its letters, so depriving the City of a central source for distributing the news; for a week thereafter the mail was disorganized, resulting in a new spate of alarmist rumours of foreign plots and arson.

Before long Gracechurch Street, Lombard Street, Cornhill and Thread-needle Street were alight and so was the Royal Exchange. In the day time the flames were less spectacular than was the immense pall of smoke that billowed over the metropolis. In *God's Terrible Voice in the City*, published in 1667, the Reverend Thomas Vincent described how 'the yellow smoke of London ascendeth into heaven, like the smoke of a great furnace; a smoke so great as darkened the sun at noon-day; if at any time the sun peeped forth, it looked red with blood'. As far as Oxford the sun was dimmed to redness, while ashes fell as far to the west as Windsor.

The king and the Duke of York rose nobly to the occasion, being continually in the City, dirty and dishevelled, fighting the flames, pulling down houses with the rest and displaying a remarkable calmness and courage that helped to still the panic and encourage action. As Dryden wrote the following year:

> *Now day appears and with the day the king,*
> *Whose early care had robbed him of his rest.*
> *Far off the cracks of falling houses ring*
> *And shrieks of subjects pierce his tender breast.*

Apart from direct, physical action, the king appointed members of the Privy Council to parts of the City with summary powers to deal with disorder, a necessary step to save innocent foreigners from violence, a typical instance of which occurred at Moorgate where a Frenchman was almost dismembered because he was thought to be carrying fireballs. They turned out to be tennis-balls. The magistrates, indeed, arrested many foreigners and imprisoned them temporarily to save them from the fury of the mob.

As he rode around on horseback, the king would scatter golden guineas from a pouch to the fire-fighters as rewards and incentives. A letter of the period tells of 'his Majesty's and the Duke of York's singular care and pains, handling

30. *Another painting of the Great Fire showing the fleeing crowds. The viewpoint from Wapping is the same as that of the painting shown in the frontispiece to this book.*

the water in buckets when they stood up to the ankles in water, and playing the engines for many hours together, as they did at the Temple and Cripplegate, which people seeing, fell to work with effect, having so good fellow labourers'.

Two important buildings were saved from the holocaust. Though its western front was damaged, Leadenhall Market on the top of the eastern breast of the City was protected through the exertions of an alderman who, like the king, scattered coins to encourage the citizens to greater effort. This was the first spot where the conflagration was halted so that East India House close by was untouched. Part of the Guildhall was also preserved thanks to its massive stonework, although all the interior was consumed, leaving only the shell standing. When the fire found it, as Vincent wrote, it appeared as 'a fearful spectacle, which stood the whole body of it together in view, for several hours together, after the fire had taken it, without flames (I suppose because the timber was such solid oak) in a bright shining coal, as if it had been a palace of gold, or a great building of burnished brass'. Thanks again to the solidity of the structure, the invaluable documents in the vaults of the Guildhall, and with them a major part of the City's history, were happily preserved.

Like Pepys, that other diarist John Evelyn, at that time in control of prisoners

31. *The Fire stimulated interest in fire-fighting appliances like this water pump shown dousing flames at the rebuilt Royal Exchange.*

of war, had watched the fire spread but, unlike Pepys, he had also made some physical effort to stay the flames when they reached Holborn. 'O the miserable and calamitous spectacle', he wrote, 'such as perhaps the whole world had not seen its like since the foundation of it: nor is it to be outdone until the world's universal conflagration. All the sky was of a fiery aspect like the top of a burning oven, and the light was seen for above forty miles round about for many nights. God grant my eyes may never behold the like, who now saw about ten thousand houses all in one flame. The noise, crackling and thunder of the impetuous flames, the shrieking of women and children, the hurry of people, and the fall of towers, houses and churches, was like an hideous storm: and the air all about was so hot and inflamed that, at the last, one was not able to approach it, so that they were forced to stand still and let the flames consume on, which they did for near two miles in length and one in breadth. The clouds of smoke also were dismal, and reached, upon computation, nearly fifty miles in length. Thus I left it this afternoon burning, a resemblance of Sodom, or the Last Day. London was, but is no more.'

As happens in all great calamities, people behaved both at their best and at their worst. Thousands fought the flames bravely, others gave succour to their neighbours and housed the dispossessed until they in their turn were forced to flee. At the height of the fire, citizens ran to the levels of Moorfields and Finsbury Fields outside the Wall to the north, an area where laundresses hung out their washing, and there they camped with whatever goods and chattels they had managed to carry with them. By the time some thirteen thousand houses had been destroyed, a hundred thousand people were on the move without food or shelter. The authorities had early banned the movement of carts but the order was soon revoked. At the gates in the Wall the jostling crowds were immense, refugees streaming out to safety and others from the Liberties and suburbs entering with carts in search of readily earned lucre or merely to loot. A carter could demand half the value of the goods he rescued and the fee for a hiring rose from ten shillings to fifty pounds.

That the weather was warm and dry was a single mitigating circumstance. Goods were carried to Lincoln's Inn Fields, Gray's Inn Fields, Hatton Garden and Covent Garden, where Trained Bands were stationed to guard them; schools and churches were opened for storage.

By the time the fire had reached Cheapside, the City's grand alley where rich merchants and goldsmiths were quartered, all money and valuables in their houses had been stored in the Tower of London, so that, although their Hall in Foster Lane was destroyed, the goldsmiths lost less than other merchants who dealt in more bulky wares. St Mary-le-Bow in Cheapside, the finest parish church in London, ranking second in importance to the cathedral as an ecclesiastical fabric (in fact, a kind of cathedral itself in being an Archbishop's Peculiar), was ruined except for its fine Norman crypt which is still in being below Wren's masterpiece. This was the church whose bells confirmed that a man was a true Cockney if born within range of their sound.

Sweeping north, the fire roared around the City's highest and most dominant building, Old St Paul's. The crypt with its four aisles, called St Faith, was being used as a parish church, serving also as the church of the Stationers' Company. There the booksellers had stored their stocks. The old cathedral seemed to be standing safely enough in the sea of fire when suddenly as darkness fell on the Tuesday evening, flying brands set the roof alight. When this collapsed, the whole edifice became a raging, greedy inferno that found nourishment in the timber scaffolding erected for the survey of the building. Molten lead from the roof poured down like water into the surrounding streets, as if, in Vincent's words, 'it had been snow before the sun'. Great stones split apart as if exploding. As Evelyn recorded, 'The stones of St Paul's flew like grenados, and the lead melted down the streets in a stream. The very pavements glowed with fiery redness, and neither horse nor man was able to tread on them'.

Filled with books valued at £150,000, the crypt had been carefully sealed but, tragically, the fire destroyed this valuable library. Various explanations of how the flames reached the vaults have been put forward, the most plausible being that the booksellers opened the doors too soon so that the air admitted ignited the piles of over-heated volumes. They burned for a week until they were no more than a great mound of ash.

Before the flames had reached St Paul's they were rushing like a torrent down Ludgate Hill. They leapt the Fleet River and began to devour Black-friars, including the parish of St Bride's and the lawless sanctuary of Alsatia. By six o'clock on the Tuesday evening they licked the walls of the Temple and consumed one of the houses of Middle Temple. There at last, and at Fetter Lane across the highway, the fire was finally stayed to the west. The old church of the Templars was barely touched thanks to the blowing up of surrounding buildings with gunpowder under the direction of the Duke of York. (Although badly damaged in the Second World War, it has been brilliantly repaired and still stands today.) Clifford's Inn, except for one build-ing, was saved, and at the Hall there the Fire Court to adjust post-Fire claims was to be held.

The fire had been spreading less rapidly on the east of the City owing to the direction of the wind. Although the Elizabethan Custom House by the river was quite destroyed the flames did not run beyond All Hallows, Barking. The Tower of London, where for a time a large quantity of gunpowder had been dangerously stored, remained untouched, and apart from the demolition of some houses there, Seething Lane where Pepys lived was unharmed. Before sunrise on Wednesday, the Pepys household had been in alarm nevertheless. 'About two in the morning my wife calls me up and tells me of new cries of "fire!" – it being come to Barking Church, which is the bottom of our lane. I up; and finding it so, resolved presently to take her away; and did, and took my gold (which was about £2,350), W. Hewer and Jane down by Poundy's boat to Woolwich. But Lord, what a sad sight it was by moonlight to see the whole City almost on fire – that you might see it plain at Woolwich, as if you were by it. There when I came, I find the gates shut, but no guard kept at

32. *Tillimans' painting of Charles II walking with his courtiers on Horse Guards Parade, Whitehall, near the Royal Palace. The Banqueting Hall is in the background.*

all; which troubled me, because of discourses now begun that there is a plot in it and that the French had done it. I got the gates open, and to Mr Sheldon's, where I locked up my gold and charged my wife and W. Hewer never to leave the room without one of them in it night nor day. So back again, by the way seeing my goods well in the lighters at Deptford and watched well by people. Home, and whereas I expected to have seen our house on fire, it now being seven o'clock, it was not. But to the Fire, and there find greater hopes than I expected; for my confidence of finding our office on fire was such, that I durst not ask anybody how it was with us, till I came and saw it not burned. But going to the fire, I find, by the blowing up of houses and the great help given by the workmen out of the king's yards, sent up by Sir W. Penn, there is a good stop given to it, as well at Mark Lane end as ours.'

Up to the top of All Hallows steeple went Pepys and there 'saw the saddest sight of desolation that I ever saw. Everywhere great fires. Oil-cellars and brimstone and other things burning. I became afeared to stay there long; and therefore down again as fast as I could, the fire being spread as far as I could see it, and to Sir W. Penn's and there eat a piece of cold meat, having eaten nothing since Sunday but the remains of Sunday's dinner. Here I met with Mr Young and Whistler; and having removed all my things, and received good hopes that the fire at our end is stopped, they and I walked into the town and find Fenchurch Street, Gracechurch Street, and Lombard Street all in dust. The Exchange a sad sight, nothing standing there of all the statues or pillars but Sir Thomas Gresham's picture in the corner. Walked into Moorfields (our feet ready to burn, walking through the town among the hot coals) and find that

33. *The Duke of York, brother of Charles II, who became James II, in a diamond etching on glass of c. 1660. He joined the king in fighting the flames.*

full of people, and poor wretches carrying their goods there, and everybody keeping his goods together by themselves (and a great blessing it is to them that it is fair weather for them to keep abroad night and day); drank there, and paid twopence for a plain penny loaf. Thence homeward, having passed through Cheapside and Newgate Market, all burned ... I also did see a poor cat taken out of a hole in the chimney joining to the wall of the Exchange, with the hair all burned off the body and yet alive. So home at night ... And I lay down and slept a good night about midnight – though when I rose, I hear that there had been a great alarm of French and Dutch being risen – which proved nothing.'

At last the fire was burning itself out. Late on the Tuesday night the high wind had veered to the south, had moderated and died. Thousands returned to the City to kill the flickering embers. 'Now they began to bestir themselves (and not till now),' wrote Evelyn, 'who till now had stood as men restrained, with their arms crossed.' The sound of explosions continued for a while to the west, and at Cripplegate arose the last violent flare. In all, the Great Fire burned for four days and nights. The citizens were hungry and exhausted, including Pepys, who was 'all dirt from top to bottom'. For some nights he was to sleep restlessly, 'much terrified with dreams of fire and falling down of houses'.

The crowds were in a frightened, aggressive and dangerous mood, and the first step the authorities knew they must take was to stem the wild rumours. The whole country was in a state of tension, fearing invasion. If London could first be calmed, tension would relax elsewhere. On Thursday, 6 September, the king rode out to Moorfields to address the homeless citizens there encamped, seeking to allay their suspicions that the fire had been caused by the plotting of the Dutch, French, Catholics or unknown fanatics. He assured them that the Fire was solely an act of God and that he would protect and care for them all like a father.

Dutchmen were, in fact, delighted by the event, regarding it as a just punishment from Heaven, but Louis XIV prohibited rejoicing in France and magnanimously offered to send relief. Before long a Committee of Inquiry was to be formed at which wild evidence would be taken, most of it clearly apocryphal, but rioting and persecution were averted.

Now the enormous task of clearance and reconstruction lay ahead.

4. *Devastation and Dreams*

The first need was to feed and shelter the homeless. The king provided army tents and ship's biscuits from the naval stores, while the City permitted the erection of temporary dwellings on the open spaces north of the Wall. Royal orders were issued to the out-parishes to provide lodgings without extortion, and to all corporate towns in the country to permit refugees to pursue their trades therein. Churches, chapels, schools and public buildings were pro-claimed open for the storage of goods and chattels that had been rescued, and temporary markets were established in the unharmed areas of the City, in the Liberties and in surrounding villages.

In the City the poorer citizens rapidly set up sheds of brick and timber on the ruins of their homes or made use of their cellars, and soon many temporary ale houses were erected among the ruins for the use of the labourers who came in daily from the suburbs to clear the rubble and douse the remaining embers. The City government was re-established in Gresham College, the Post House or Office in Bishopsgate, the Custom House in Mark Lane and the Law Courts in the Strand. Private enterprise set up an office where people could leave their new addresses in order to keep contact with friends, relatives or customers.

Removal of debris on the Bridge, accomplished at night by torchlight, was the first act of clearance so that communications with the south bank could be renewed as soon as possible. Troops marched in from the home counties to help prevent further outbreaks of fire, and on the Sunday following the Fire, rain fell at last, bringing further help. Yet small fires continued for some weeks, and even a deluge of rain lasting ten days during October failed to extinguish all the hidden flames; indeed, as late as 16 March the following year Pepys recorded that he had noticed smoke issuing from some cellars in the devastated City.

On 7 September, the Friday after the Fire, Evelyn explored the wreckage: 'I was infinitely concerned to find that goodly church, St Paul's, a sad ruin, and that beautiful portico – for structure comparable to any in Europe, and not long before repaired by the late king – now rent in pieces . . . Thus lay in ashes that most venerable church, one of the ancientest pieces of early piety in the Christian world; and so indeed lay nearly an hundred more . . . The people, who now walked about the ruins appeared like men in some dismal desert, or rather in some great city laid waste by an impetuous and cruel enemy: to which was added the stench that came from some poor creatures' bodies, beds and other combustible goods . . . Nor was I yet able to pass through any of the narrower streets, but kept the widest. The ground and air, smoke and fiery

34. *A silver tankard commemorating
the Great Fire.*

vapour, continued so intense that my hair was almost singed and my feet unsufferably sore.'

Evelyn then went towards Islington and Highgate, 'where one might have seen two hundred thousand people, of all ranks and degrees, dispersed and lying alongside their heaps of what they could save from the *Incendium*, deploring their loss, and yet, though ready to perish for hunger and destitution, not asking one penny for relief – which to me appeared a stranger sight than any I had yet beheld. His Majesty and Council indeed took all imaginable care for their relief, by proclamation for the country people to come in and refresh them with provisions.'

Yet the speed of rehabilitation was remarkable; within less than a week the open fields around the City were deserted and nearly everyone was under cover of some kind, either in new mushroom villages of sheds and tents, or by 'doubling up' in the houses in the Liberties or packing into inns and places of public entertainment. In the common calamity mutual aid abounded. But

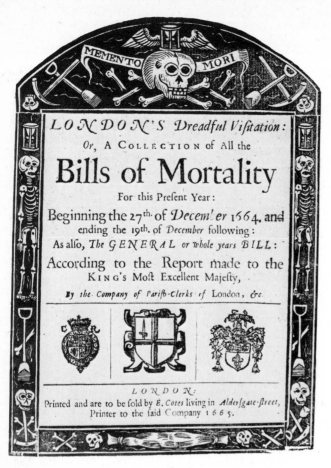

LONDON'S Dreadful Visitation: Or, A Collection of All the

Bills of Mortality

For this Present Year:

Beginning the 27th. of December 1664. and ending the 19th. of December following:

As also, The GENERAL or whole years BILL:

According to the Report made to the KING's Most Excellent Majesty,

By the Company of Parish-Clerks of London, &c.

LONDON:

Printed and are to be sold by E. Cotes living in Aldersgate-street, Printer to the said Company 1 6 6 5.

35. *The title page of a collection of London's Bills of Mortality of 1665.*

for many the months that followed the Fire were miserable, the torrential rains of October being followed by winter months that were the coldest on record, so cold that the Thames froze solid. Apart from the inadequacy of temporary shelters, rents and the price of coal were hugely inflated. Significantly the customary bonfires were not burned on 5 November 1666; the situation was too grim for jollity and no doubt for the moment everyone had had enough of flames and ashes.

The scene of desolation across the incinerated corpse of a town, where skeletal towers rose here and there from the rubble, was horrifying. 'I can but say this,' wrote a contemporary, 'that there is nothing but stones and rubbish, and all exposed to the open air, so that you may see from one end of the City to the other. You can compare London (were it not for the rubbish) to nothing more than an open field.' So great and traumatic a catastrophe as the Fire of London becomes, in time, recorded not only in local and national annals and history books but all over the world; significantly after the terrible Tokyo earthquake of 1923, the Japanese sent to know how London had met her calamity in 1666.

The Fire caused surprisingly few deaths. The Bills of Mortality computed that the number was only six, but that is probably too low an estimate. No doubt far more people lost their lives in the ruined city immediately after the Fire, either from tumbling walls or from footpads, some of them inmates of prisons who had broken gaol, and swarmed among the ruins in search of plunder in the cellars. One James Hickes wrote in a letter three months after the Fire: 'There are many people found murdered and carried into the vaults amongst the ruins, as three last night, as I hear, and it is supposed by hasty fellows that cry "Do you want light?" and carry links; and that when they catch a man single, whip into a vault with him, knock him down, strip him from top to toe, blow out their links and leave the persons for dead . . . For want of good watches, no person dare, after the close of the evening, pass the streets among the ruins.'

36. *Gresham House in Bishopsgate, which the Fire did not touch, as seen in 1739. Here the Common Council and the Royal Exchange acquired temporary accommodation after the Fire.*

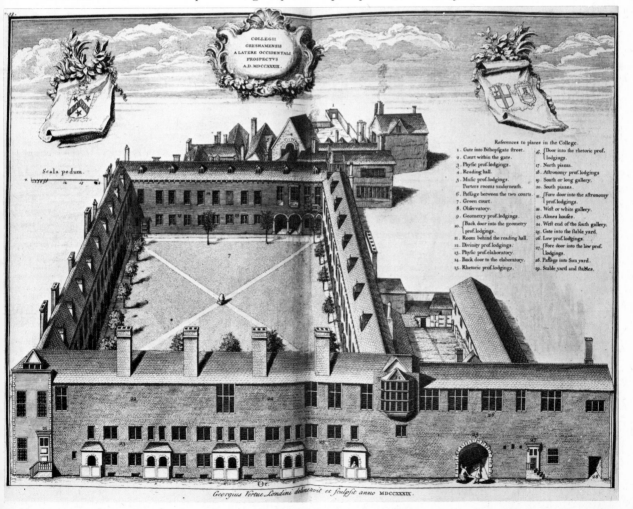

After dark the City gates were closed and this helped to preserve some order, while on 3 November the Lord Mayor issued a proclamation for the punishment 'of vagrants and sturdy beggars, loose and idle persons, who greatly abound, wandering in and about the streets of London and amongst the ruins of this city', the aldermen being commanded to set up stocks and whipping posts for their punishment when caught in their wards.

The loss of property through the Fire was enormous, and was particularly distressing to house-owners at a time when no fire insurance existed. A final count by the City Surveyors gave the following figures:

   373 acres burnt within the walls
    63 acres 3 roods without the walls
    87 parish churches, besides chapels, burnt
13,200 houses burnt in over 400 streets and courts
    75 acres 3 roods still standing within the walls unburnt
    11 parish churches without the walls yet standing.

The entire area destroyed was equivalent to an oblong measuring a mile and a half by half a mile, or three-quarters of a square mile. In fact, of the hundred and seven churches of the City only eighty-four were entirely destroyed, three were partly burnt and later repaired, while twenty-two were unharmed. Of those destroyed Wren was to rebuild fifty-one. Of the Halls of the Livery Companies, forty-four were burnt and seven survived, although none of those seven exist today in pre-Fire form.

The Royal Exchange, centre of business and foreign trade and the heart of the mercantile city, was in ruins, but happily in the untouched area to the east stood the great mansion of Sir Thomas Gresham in Bishopsgate around a wide courtyard. It contained Gresham College and was held in joint trust by

37. Hollar's engraving of Arundel House in the Strand in 1646. Here the Royal Society was given a home when moved from Gresham House after the Fire.

38. London Bridge and the frozen Thames in 1677. A winter like this followed the Fire, adding to the discomforts of the homeless.

the City Corporation and the Gresham Company, mercers. There the Lord Mayor and other homeless dignitaries were given lodgings and there the Common Council held its first meeting on the Monday after the Fire. So Gresham House served temporarily as both Exchange and Guildhall. To make more room the Royal Society was ejected and was found new accommodation at Arundel House in the Strand, a palace owned by Henry Howard, a newly elected member of the Society who was to become the sixth Duke of Norfolk. Within the walls of the gutted Guildhall, the debris was cleared and a temporary wooden structure raised wherein the courts could be held in their usual place.

There was some talk of moving the capital entire to some other city, and York had hopes that it might be chosen. In the event London re-established itself bravely in its old position and carried on with that talent for rapid improvisation that is one of the more admirable traits of the English character. Dr Sprat, later Bishop of Rochester, paid a tribute to London's citizens in their hour of trial: 'They beheld the ashes of their houses, gates and temples without the least pusillanimity. If philosophers had done this, it had well become their profession of wisdom; if gentlemen, the nobleness of their breeding and blood would have required it; but that such greatness of heart should have been found among the obscure multitude is no doubt one of the most honourable events that ever happened. A new City is to be built, on the most advantageous seat of all Europe for trade and command.' And Henry Oldenburg wrote to Robert Boyle on 10 September: 'The citizens, instead of complaining, discourse almost of nothing but of a survey for rebuilding the City with bricks and large streets.' The stupor of shock was soon overcome.

Sympathy for the City's plight arose not only all over the country but also abroad. Many boroughs, counties and individuals sent financial aid to a Lord Mayor's fund; even poor Ireland offered both cash and cattle. The king ordered that 10 September be a day of fasting on which 'to implore the mercies of God, that it would please him to pardon the crying sins of this nation, those especially which have drawn down this last and heavy punishment upon us'. He com-

39. *The wax effigy of Charles II in that remarkable miniature Madame Tussauds in the crypt of Westminster Abbey.*

manded that collections be taken in every church of the realm to help sufferers and also from door to door. The order helped to reduce the hysteria and para-noia of supposed foreign plotting, but the polemics were also typical of the times. Evelyn, for example, considered that the Fire was highly deserved 'for our prodigious ingratitude, burning lusts, dissolute court, profane and abomin-able lives'. Most people remained unmoved by this kind of talk, having had sufficient from the Puritans, and continued to act in a practical way on the assumption that, according to all known experience, God tends to help those who help themselves.

The immense, filthy, sweaty job of clearing the rubble now began. The chaotic situation was soon under control and provisional action was under-taken with commendable despatch and common sense. The first order of the Council was to direct property owners to clear away the rubbish on their sites and to pile up bricks and stones within a fortnight, not only to aid communica-tions but to enable a full survey to be undertaken.

With ill-considered enthusiasm, one house-owner began to rebuild his property at Blackfriars a week after the Fire was out, just as a Royal Proclama-tion, issued on 13 September, prohibited any building of a permanent nature until general regulations had been published; any new building that arose would be at once demolished by order, and the builder punished. It was a sensible proclamation. Charles II once more emerges as arguably the wisest and deservedly the most popular of all English monarchs – humane, intelligent, courteous, affable, tolerant, merry and as wily as his position required, a great but attractive personality who never lost the common touch. His features can be seen today as though in the flesh with penetrating, humorous eyes, gay-dog moustache, and veined nose in that remarkable miniature Madame Tussauds to be found in the crypt of Westminster Abbey.

The king promised no needless delays. 'If any considerable number of men (for it is impossible to comply with the humour of every particular man) shall address themselves to the Court of Aldermen, and manifest to them in what places their ground lies upon which they design to build, they shall in a short time receive such order and direction for their proceeding therein, that they shall have no cause to complain.' The king desired that 'this our native city', with the citizens' help, should rise again 'making it rather appear to the world as purged with fire (in how lamentable a manner soever) to a wonderful beauty and comeliness, than consumed by it'.

One clause in the proclamation was of great importance, not only as a precaution against the outbreak of fires in the future but as an aid to producing a homogeneous vernacular style: 'No man whatsoever shall presume to erect any house or building, great or small, but of brick or stone.' All 'eminent and notorious streets' were to be widened both to help traffic flow and to reduce

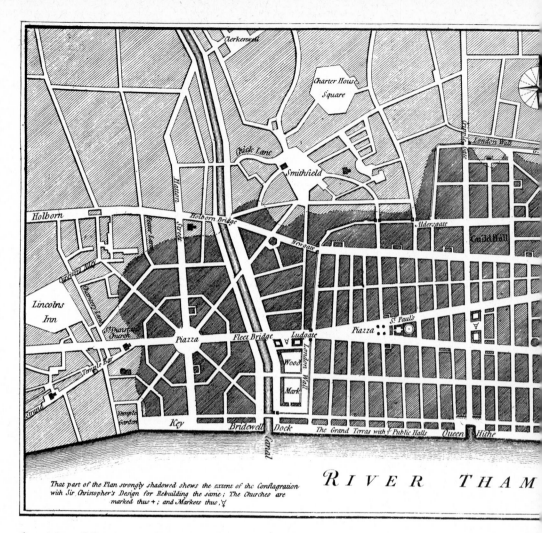

That part of the Plan strongly shadowed shews the extent of the Conflagration with Sir Christopher's Design for Rebuilding the same; The Churches are marked thus +; and Markets thus.

the risks of fires spreading, while no lanes should be too steep or narrow for easy passage. A quay would extend along the whole length of the riverside. All trades that produced smoke and stink should be removed elsewhere to chosen places. At the same time, no man's right of property would be sacrificed to public convenience. There was some grumbling, for London people had always resented royal interference with their liberties, but most men realized that firm central control was necessary under the egregious circumstances.

Where was Christopher Wren during the Fire? I can find no evidence that he was in or near London when it was at its height; presumably he was at Oxford. He was certainly in London as soon as the Fire was over, when his small figure could have been seen scrambling among the ruins at some personal hazard to make a rough survey of the devastated area. He at once set to work and with incredible speed drew out his famous street plan for a new model City which he presented to the king and Council on 11 September, only six days after the

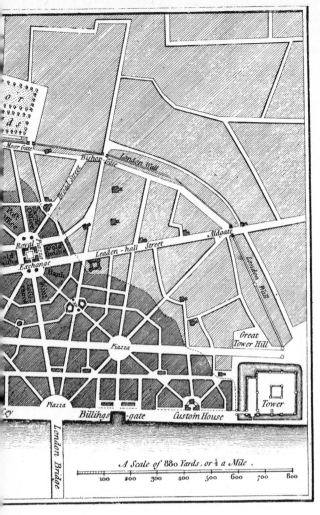

40. *Wren's great plan for a new City.*

Fire had died down. It was carefully drawn and measured 2 feet 3 inches by 1 foot 2 inches.

It was a splendid, coherent, well-reasoned plan, somewhat baroque in its bold, straight streets running to monuments or open places of geometric outlines, in its symmetries, and in its reticulation at least of the narrower streets. There were continental precedents for a system of radiating throughfares: the Rome of Sixtus V, the Paris of Henry IV, and French formal gardens. The block system Wren adopted is familiar today in American cities, though its antecedents go back at least to ancient Rome, as anyone who has visited the ruined cities of Pompeii and Herculaneum will know. Fixed marks were taken at the existing City gates, at the highways outside the burnt area, and at St Paul's and the Royal Exchange which would be renewed on their old sites. This is something of a failing in the plan in that the corners at the crossings of the new streets show hardly a single right angle anywhere. Barely any account is taken of the old street jumble and the lay-out is ruthlessly despotic towards private ownership of the old plots. That is why it proved unacceptable in spite of its practicality and grandeur. As Sir Nathaniel Hobart, Master in Chancery, observed: 'The rebuilding of the City will not be so difficult as the satisfying of all interests, there being so many proprietors.'

The chief aims of Wren's plan were five: first, to let the Royal Exchange stand on its old site as an isolated building set in a wide forum to form 'the nave or centre of the town'; secondly, to give the new St Paul's Cathedral, also on its old site, the dramatic significance the capital city required with a triumphal arch in honour of the king as founder of New London on the axis approach at Ludgate, the approach road being ninety feet wide and funnelling out up the hill towards the cathedral where it would bifurcate – on the north towards the Royal Exchange and to the south right along in a dead straight line towards a group of trees on Tower Hill; thirdly, to improve communications with London Bridge by means of four converging streets, one of them running straight along to the Royal Exchange; fourthly, to clear the riverside all the way from the Tower to the Temple, and erect on that stretch a broad, open public quay forty feet wide – an idea no doubt inspired by Wren's fresh memory of the Paris quays along the Seine; fifthly, to clear the Fleet River, now no more than a stinking, open sewer, and to turn it, in the Dutch manner, into a straight, clean canal, a hundred and twenty feet wide with quays ninety feet wide on each side.

A number of new churches would be built at various articulated spots along the main streets with ample space around them, and they would be designed, according to *Parentalia*, 'according to the best forms for capacity and hearing, adorned with useful porticos, and lofty ornamental towers and steeples, in the greater parishes'.

To the north and west, the old City, untouched by the Fire, would be left in its original form with suitable new road linkages. Easy access from the whole City would be given to the riverside quay, along which would lie four indented harbours – at Billingsgate, Dowgate, Queenhithe and Bridewell. Towards the Tower, along the riverside, a new Custom House would be built on the old site.

Around the wide forum of the Royal Exchange (built with double porticos) would stand the most important buildings of the City: Excise Office, Mint, Goldsmiths' Hall (centre of banking), and a new concept, generated by the Fire, an Insurance Office. The Guildhall would be moved south-west from its old site, and facing the square around it would stand the new halls of the City Companies. To the west, Fleet Street, now widened to ninety feet, would run through a great piazza. All the new streets, in fact, would be of three standard widths: ninety, sixty and thirty feet. All the old, irregular and narrow alleys, and the small green spaces ('unnecessary vacuities' in Wren's phrase) would be banished. The picturesque medieval casbah would exist no more.

41. *The ruins of Old St Paul's after the Fire showing the Italianate west porch by Inigo Jones.*

The lay-out was masterly. It opened up the whole City and would thereby have rendered it safe from all future pestilence and fire. More than two and a half centuries later, the great Edwin Chadwick, battling at the Board of Health almost alone against public apathy and vested interests to make the Great Wen healthier at a time when cholera had become endemic in London, expressed the fervent wish that Wren's plan had been adopted because in his estimate it would have reduced the mortality rate of all succeeding generations of city dwellers by a third.

The king was impressed by Wren's plan, for, to quote again from *Parentalia*, he was among those 'intelligent persons who thought it highly requisite, the City in the restoration should rise with that beauty, by the straightness and regularity of buildings, and convenience for commerce, by the well disposing of streets and public places, and the opening of wharves, etc. which the excellent situation, wealth and grandeur of the metropolis of England did justly deserve; in respect also of the rank she bore with all other trading cities of the World, of which though she was before one of the richest in estate and dowry, yet unquestionably the least beautiful.'

42. *Charles II by an unknown artist.*

Wren's son in his filial piety extolled the plan: 'The practicality of this whole scheme, without loss to any man, or infringement of any property, was that time demonstrated, and all material objections fully weighed, and answered: the only, and, as it happened, insurmountable difficulty remaining, was the obstinate averseness to great part of the citizens to alter their old properties, and to recede from building their houses again on the old ground and foundations; as also, the distrust in many, and unwillingness to give up their properties, though for a time only, into the hands of public trustees, or commissioners, till they might be dispensed to them again, with more advantage to themselves, than otherwise was possible to be effected . . . although few proprietors should happen to have been seated again, directly upon the very same ground they had possessed before the Fire, yet no man would have been thrust any considerable distance from it, but had been placed at least as conveniently, and sometime more so, to their own trades than before. By these means, the opportunity, in a great degree, was lost, of making the new City the most magnificent, as well as commodious for health and trade of any upon earth; and the surveyor being thus confined and cramped in his designs, it required no small labour and skill, to model the City in the manner it has since appeared . . . The Fire of London, furnished the most perfect occasion that can ever happen in any city, to rebuild it with pomp and regularity: this, Wren foresaw, and, as we are told, offered a scheme for that purpose, which would have made it the wonder of the world.'

Wren's plan was later engraved, the earliest print by Halsberg being published in 1721 (reissued 1744). John Gwynne published one in 1749 though it is not precisely as Wren drew it, and its note that the scheme was 'approved by Parliament and unhappily defeated by Faction' is untrue.

The colossal scheme, being only a rapid sketch, had faults. Its cost would have been enormous and it would have taken far too long a time to accomplish when rapid reconstruction was urgent. The whole burnt area was seen as a huge vacant site and all the old associations of place would have been eliminated. All the ancient parish boundaries, some going back to Norman times, would have vanished and not one of the old thoroughfares would have been retained. The twenty-one miles of new roads would have run across old filled-in basements and cellars, all the buildings would have required new foundations, many of them deep, and existing water pipes and courses would have been useless. St Paul's Cathedral would have been invisible from the east and the acute or obtuse angles of the street corners would have made awkward building sites and turnings.

Wren's plan was the first to be presented but a few days later several others were being considered by king and Council. None could compare in imagination and intelligence with Wren's, but they are not without interest. John Evelyn presented his on 13 September. It showed some similarities to Wren's, including the riverside quay and the Fleet Canal, the great piazza with radiating streets to the west through which ran the Strand, the streets converging towards a place at the bridgehead, and St Paul's on its old site set in a new open space. As Wren had also proposed, the old houses on London Bridge would be removed. Unlike Wren, however, Evelyn brought the Royal Exchange down to the riverside behind the new quay at the spot where Cannon Street Station is now, and where at one time the Steelyard, headquarters of the Hanseatic League or Easterlings (hence Sterling) once stood. All main streets were one hundred feet wide, ten feet more than Wren's, and where they opened out into places, grand sculptured fountains spouted water. And Evelyn placed all burial grounds, in the hygienic Roman manner, in a line outside the Wall. His plan was less drastic than Wren's and preserved more ancient sites of antiquarian interest; twenty-five new churches, for instance, retained their old positions.

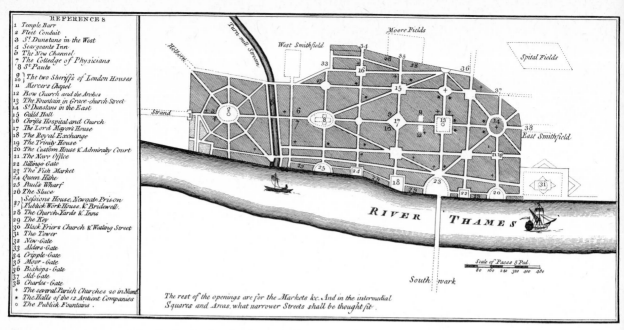

REFERENCES
1 Temple Barr
2 Fleet Conduit
3 St Dunstans in the West
4 Seargeants Inn
5 The New Channel
7 The Colledge of Physicians
8 St Pauls
9 } The two Sheriffs of London Houses
10
11 Mercer's Chapel
12 Bow Church and the Arches
13 The Fountain in Grace-church Street
14 St Dunstans in the East
15 Guild Hall
16 Christs Hospital and Church
17 The Lord Mayors House
18 The Royal Exchange
19 The Trinity House
20 The Custom House & Admiralty Court
21 The Navy Office
22 Billings Gate
23 The Fish Market
24 Queen Hithe
25 Pauls Wharf
26 The Sluce
27 } Sessions House, Newgate Prison
   Publick Work House, &c Bridewell.
28 The Church-Yards & Inns
29 The Key
30 Black Friers Church & Watling Street
31 The Tower
32 New-Gate
33 Alders-Gate
34 Cripple-Gate
35 Moor-Gate
36 Bishops-Gate
37 Ald-Gate
38 Charles-Gate
+ The several Parish Churches 20 in Numb.
* The Halls of the 12 Antient Companies
o The Publick Fountains.

The rest of the openings are for the Markets &c. And in the intermedial Squares and Areas, what narrower Streets shall be thought fit.

43. *John Evelyn's plan for the new City.*

As Evelyn wrote in a letter: 'Dr Wren got a start of me, but both of us did coincide so frequently that his Majesty was not displeased'. But his plan lacked the verve of Wren's. Dr Robert Hooke, Professor of Mathematics at Gresham College and a friend of Wren, also presented a plan. It was practical but rigid with a grid-iron street lay-out; the philistine City fathers preferred it to those of Wren and Evelyn, and it may later have influenced them in giving Hooke the job of City Surveyor. There were other plans too, including one by Peter Mills, the then City Surveyor, and two by Richard Newcourt, the map maker. None were in the end accepted.

A Captain Valentine Knight sent in a daring idea for a canal, thirty feet wide, to run in an arc through the City from Billingsgate to the Fleet River at Holborn Bridge, which he claimed could bring huge profits to the Crown. The cunning king, in an unkind and ungrateful mood, ordered Knight's arrest, thus reassuring the citizens that he was not the kind of ruler who would manipulate a public calamity in such a way.

As perfectionists we may regret that Wren's plan was not applied. It is to Wren's credit that he accepted the hard facts of the situation without bitterness and contributed his best to the situation of compromise. The chief difficulty was less the avarice and suspicion of the individualistic citizens than the need to speed reconstruction so that morale and trade could recover as soon as possible – no small consideration by king and parliament since the City was a valuable source of revenue. The second problem at a time when a costly war was being waged against France and the States General, was money. A drastic replanning, with its time-wasting adjustments, would have delayed revival considerably and might even have forced the removal of England's main port and centre of commerce to some other place. Citizens were forced to rebuild in a hurry with little ready-made legislation or administration to help them in an enormous and difficult task. Moreover, the enforcement of a complete baroque re-planning was out of ideological key with the times in England, and out of key too with the English temperament and constitution, for it had a tyrannical aspect that was possible only in countries where monarchy was absolute and financial resources lavish, a state that did not exist in England as the king's tact makes evident. The king could advise, encourage and propose but his powers were limited.

London has always been, and remains, the Tolerant City, and therein lie both its discontents and its charms. Even today, in spite of the faceless building horrors erected here during the past few decades with all their rude manners, not least towards Wren's cathedral, the City still retains many picturesque delights and surprises in unpremeditated vistas, intimate alleys and hidden green spaces, the legacy of the medieval muddle that was retained to a considerable extent in post-Fire planning. Life, after all, is never very orderly so that towns, if they are to be living communities, can never be orderly either; they must be continually adapted to changing circumstances. A town built all at one time as the conception of a single mind tends to be depressingly sterile and cannot be readily adapted to life's vagaries and uncertainties. Nor does it possess those links with the past that make a town tolerable to live in by producing scenes compounded of the styles of different ages to delight the eye and the imagination.

In that thorough record, *The Rebuilding of London after the Great Fire* (1940), T. F. Reddaway takes an emphatic stand with which it is hard to disagree: 'Seen in isolation, and not as an incident in the course of events, it [Wren's plan] has bred the story of a great and neglected opportunity. The documents tell a different tale. In them he [Wren] acquires the credit for a new work, the Fleet Canal, but ceases to be the rejected creator of a miraculous new city. They show no hero, no presiding genius. The focal point is the struggle of the community to survive destruction. Their mass, often unindexed, seldom calendared, sometimes unsorted, gradually yields a picture of difficulties faced and surmounted. In spite of mistakes and misconceptions, the splendour of the community's achievement is their only final conclusion.' No hero, no presiding genius – except possibly the king.

In spite of the age-old and restricting problem of reconciling private and public interest, the achievements in the rebuilding of London, so greatly aided by Wren's adaptable genius, were, indeed, remarkable enough.

5. *Realities of Reconstruction*

So London was not to be rebuilt on a grand new master plan; the old pattern of streets was to be retained, but with a number of significant improvements.

At the beginning of October, barely a month after the Fire, a rebuilding commission of six men was formed, the three architects Wren, Hugh May and Roger Pratt being appointed by the king and Privy Council, and Robert Hooke, Peter Mills and John Oliver by the City. Wren's experience of building was still limited but his brilliance and competence were so obvious that in 1669, aged only thirty-seven, he was appointed Surveyor of the King's Works in succession to Sir John Denham, soldier and poet, who died that year, a post he was to retain for fifty years. Thus, as director of all royal buildings and established in his new premises in Scotland Yard, off Whitehall, he became the most important architect in the country.

Among the original six men of the commission, Wren and Hooke dominated the rebuilding of the City for three decades. Both being scientists and architects, they talked the same language and worked well together in daily communication, like senior and junior partner. Hooke was responsible for a number of buildings in the City, and in some of the new churches it is hard to tell which of the two was chief designer. An excellent administrator and surveyor, Hooke was energetic, thorough and honest, but he was no architectural genius and in all the major works Wren's hand is unmistakable. Wren certainly liked and respected him and accepted many of his ideas. The Fire Monument, in fact, was mainly Hooke's work and he was also responsible for both the Bedlam Hospital in Moorfields and for the Royal College of Physicians in Warwick Lane with its spacious courtyard and strange domed lecture hall and entrance, a building that survived until the late nineteenth century.

The amount of other architectural work Wren achieved after the Fire, apart from his City buildings, is astonishing. And to that work must also be added

44. *Entrance to the Fleet Canal from the Thames, revealing the urbane, brick-and-stone style of the rebuilt City.*

the many administrative, routine tasks demanded of the king's surveyor as well as his continuing interest for the rest of his life in the affairs of the Royal Society. He even had time to meet his friends for lively discourse, often in some coffee house. Hooke's diary reveals, for example, that in 1676 when Wren was at his busiest with new buildings, he entertained Hooke, Aubrey and three other Fellows of the Royal Society, and they talked about such diverse matters as 'petrifaction of bodies, about plaisters, about framing glass, form of arch, light gold statues, staining marble, filligree sodering with bran, about printing stuffs and gilding stuffs, about Dr Moor's notions, about ghosts and spirits'.

Among major buildings in the country designed by Wren after the Fire must be noted the beautiful chapel range at Emmanuel College and the noble library of Trinity College, both at Cambridge, the gentlemanly Chelsea Hospital and large parts of Greenwich Hospital, the eccentric Royal Observatory at Greenwich, Kensington Palace, Hampton Court Palace, Abingdon Town Hall, and other smaller works such as the Tom Tower at Oxford and the grand, elaborate gateway at Plymouth. There were also huge projects on the drawing board including a vast new palace at Winchester that was never completed, as well as the one at Whitehall. He was concerned also with the rehabilitating of both Westminster Abbey and Salisbury Cathedral.

A number of country houses have been attributed to Wren, but mostly without good reason for he was never a serious domestic architect. Amidst all this activity Wren had time to serve for four years as a council member of the Hudson's Bay Company and on three occasions as Member of Parliament for Old Windsor and later for a spell as Member for Weymouth; although a Royalist, he was not very politically minded and his main concern as a Member was to guard and further his work on St Paul's and other building concerns.

The first Act for rebuilding the City, after the debate on principles had abated and the inevitable had been accepted, was passed in 1667. It was short, practical, clear and sensible. Pepys recorded his reaction on reading it: 'I pray to God that I may live to see it built in that manner.' As an old Londoner he knew well enough where the shoe pinched.

The first need, however, was to obtain surveys, this time drawn, not in the old pictorial style of Agas, but in a modern scientific and accurate way. The first plan was apparently prepared in this way by John Leake and other surveyors by order of the Corporation, probably to a large scale. It has not been found but that it was made is evident from an engraved plan, the only known copy of which is preserved in the Crace Collection of the British Museum; its title reads: 'An exact survey of the Streets, Lanes and Churches contained within the ruines of the City of London first described in six Plats by John Leake (and other surveyors) in Decr. anno 1666 . . . reduced here into one entire plat by John Leake, the City Wall being added also . . . Wenceslas Hollar fecit 1667'. The scale of this engraving is 300 feet to the inch and the whole measures 33 inches by 21½ inches. It is a fine work and is interesting in that the burnt parts show only the street lines in the new manner while the unharmed parts are shown in the old way as a prospect. (Another engraving of Leake's survey to a scale of 150 feet to the inch was published by Vertue in 1723.) The Corporation also appointed John Ogilby and William Morgan, sworn surveyors, to plot out the properties, and they made a plan drawn to the large scale of 100 feet to the inch to show every street, court and building in a very accurate way; no doubt this was the plan that proved of most use in the rebuilding. As the copies in the Crace Collection and at the Guildhall reveal, it measures 8 feet 5 inches by 4 feet 7 inches and is in twenty sheets. A comparative map of London before the Fire is Faithorne and Newcourt's of 1658 which is in the British Museum.

An important clause in the Rebuilding Act proposed the setting up of a Court of Fire Judges to deal with property ownership and settle disputes

45. *Sir Matthew Hale, Lord Chief Baron, who presided over the Court that settled property disputes after the Fire.*

46. *A London coffee house, c. 1700. In such meeting places news could be exchanged, business transacted and property disputes amicably settled out of court.*

between landlords and tenants. The court was soon established in the Hall of Clifford's Inn; it worked splendidly and greatly speeded the restoration of the City. The judgements of the court were final, though subject to appeal to a special court of seven judges, and the court had power to cancel all existing agreements and covenants, many of which, with title deeds, had been burnt in the lawyers' chambers. The whole intricate business of rehabilitation was thus mercifully simplified at a sweep. A tenant could appear before the court without legal charge. If both landlord and tenant were ruined, then any sites not built upon after three years were, after nine months notice, to be appropriated by the City Corporation and sold to those who were able to build upon them, the proceeds being handed over to the original owners of the sites. It was an honest court presided over by the Puritan sage, Sir Matthew Hale, the Lord Chief Baron, who drafted the Act. As a friend wrote of him: 'He was the great pillar for the rebuilding of London. By his prudence and justice he removed a multitude of grave impediments.'

A typical judgement of the Fire Court is summarized by Bell in *The Great Fire of London*. 'Thomas Manley, petitioner, demised a house in St Swithin's Lane to William Hickman, for 21 years from Michaelmas, 1663, at £14 annual rental and without fine, the tenant covenanting to repair. Manley also owned the adjoining house, and both were burnt. Hickman declined to accept any terms to rebuild, alleging that by reason of losses sustained by the Fire he was utterly incapacitated from so doing, and he prayed to be permitted to surrender his lease. Manley desired a contribution from his tenant in respect of failure under the covenant. Ordered, that Hickman surrender the lease, contribute to petitioner £30 in satisfaction of his share of the loss to be borne by the Fire, to be paid within six months, and that he be discharged of all other liabilities.'

Right up to 29 September 1672, when the court, after two periods of extension, made its last judgement, hundreds of disputes were thus rapidly settled, and as the court's practice became known and gained public confidence, a far greater number were amicably settled out of court. So effective was the court

47. *View to the north-west from the end of the Custom House Quay by London Bridge after its houses had been removed in the early 1760s. Wren's Magnus Martyr Church is on the right, and Fishmongers' Hall is in the middle distance with the dome of St Paul's beyond it.*

48. *Edward Jerman's Fishmongers' Hall, the first of the City Halls to be rebuilt after the Fire. It faced the river just west of London Bridge conveniently near to Billingsgate.*

that the Common Council of the City commissioned Michael Wright to paint the portraits of the twenty-two judges as an act of gratitude – a commission first offered to Lely who seems to have been too busy painting the king's mistresses and other notabilities in his studio to have time to attend the judges in their chambers.

The Rebuilding Act of 1667, together with the additional tidying-up Act of 1670, covered some changes to, and widening of, the old streets, important provisions for the riverside quay and the Fleet Canal, and firm guidance on sizes, materials and construction of the new houses to which builders and owners had to conform. Thames Street was to be widened below London Bridge and all the land from there down to the river was to be raised three feet to prevent flooding and reduce the steep declivities of the river approaches. A straight new thoroughfare would be opened up from the Guildhall to the Thames, while Fish Street Hill, running to the Bridge, would be widened and so would other streets such as the east end of Cheapside, the Poultry, Ludgate Hill, and Newgate Street. The Corporation would have the right to enlarge other streets, courts and lanes 'in such a manner as there shall be cause, and by and with the approbation of his Majesty and not otherwise.' (The king, indeed, had offered a number of intelligent ideas when the Rebuilding Acts were being drafted and he retained a lively and constructive interest in the City's reconstruction – more concerned with major principles and schemes perhaps than Wren himself who came to concentrate his energies on his cathedral and churches.)

Some of the large water conduits were to be moved from the middle of the streets and placed more conveniently where they would not impede traffic, streets were to be drained to the Thames and noisome and perilous trades were prohibited in the main streets. An important provision of the first Rebuilding Act was the nomination of commissioners for sewers and paving who would exercise authority for seven years or until rebuilding had been completed, a great sanitary benefit that replaced the old and inadequate local control by each ward. The second Act extended the commissioners' powers in perpetuity, although their full powers were to last only until 1898. Under the Commission, a Fellowship of Carmen cleaned the streets and carted filth and rubbish away to laystalls. So the City acquired its first health authority.

The second Rebuilding Act authorized the construction of the Thames quay as envisaged in the master plans of both Wren and Evelyn to provide a useful, commodious and dignified river front. This was in the end only partially achieved by making some encroachments upon the foreshore. Ogilby's map of 1677 reveals its existence in part with many warehouses standing well back

49. Wren's Custom House built of stone-dressed brickwork, the first public building to be re-erected after the Fire. It was burned down forty-seven years later.

from the river, with good wharfage at Dowgate, at Puddle Dock and east of the
mouth of the Fleet. Just west of London Bridge the map shows the new Fishmongers' Hall completed in 1671 to the pleasant pedimented brick design of
Edward Jerman (rebuilt as we now see it in 1833 when Rennie's new London
Bridge replaced the old structure). By the river, further to the east, is shown the
rebuilt Custom House, the first public building to be erected after the Fire, also
finished in 1671, and important as a major source of revenue. *Parentalia*
attributes its design wholly to Wren but he may have collaborated in it with
Hugh May, King's Paymaster of the Works and later Controller of the Works.
It was burned down after only forty-seven years of life but two contemporary
engravings show how it looked, a dignified if austere piece of brick dressed
with stone, with side wings forming a wide courtyard facing the quay, the
walls being relieved by Tuscan and Ionic pilasters. The west end was elevated on
columns to form a piazza and the whole possessed a Dutch flavour. It seems to
have worked well for its purpose.

50. *The Master, Wardens and Court of Assistants of the Worshipful Company of Joiners
and Ceilers discuss the plans for their new Hall.*

In the end there was to be no fully continuous 'fair key or wharf'. Although not the splendid architectural feature Wren could have made it, nor lined with many of the City Halls as the king had envisaged it, some improvements were brought to the old irregular confusion and they lasted for over a century. But encroachments of cranes and sheds soon began and were too readily tolerated, perhaps because the cost of compensation would have been high and because increasing trade enforced provisional adjustments. While the second Act authorized the building of the quay, the first had only implied its establishment in that 'no house, outhouse or other building whatsoever (cranes and sheds for the present use only excepted) shall be built or erected within the distance of forty foot of such part of any wall, key or wharf as bounds the River Thames from Tower Wharf to London Bridge and from London Bridge to the Temple Stairs . . . before the four and twentieth day of March [1669]'. In spite of this order, only eight months after the statutory time for clearing the riverside above London Bridge had expired, Wren reported to the king: 'Everywhere enclosed and encumbered with pales or brick walls, irregular houses and buildings, piles of timber, billetts, faggots and heaps of coals, many boarded sheds and several great laystalls . . . the old towers of Baynard's Castle . . . yet standing'. The authorities seem to have been lax.

The other important proposal, that for the conversion of the stinking ditch of the Fleet River into a straight, wide and navigable canal with quays running for half a mile up to Holborn Bridge in an orderly Dutch manner was accomplished with great difficulty by 1674, thanks largely to the unstinted and dedicated efforts of the contractor, Thomas Fitch. Its attractive entrance from the river has been recorded in a delightful painting by Samuel Scott, which also shows the new type of brick house.

The Fleet Canal never really took. Too few merchants acquired storage space or houses to make the scheme financially viable, and the wharves became used illicitly for parking carts and coaches, for stacking timber, and for dumping rubbish. Coachmakers used the broad spaces of the quays as repairing grounds, stonecutters worked on them, while in one place the keeper of the Mermaid Tavern set up alfresco benches and tables to increase his custom. The quays became traffic routes so that the pavements were broken and the roofs of the storage vaults below them were in danger of collapse, and within a few years the canal itself was as choked and noisome as the old river had been, being thus described in 1710 by *The Tatler*:

> *Sweepings from butchers' stalls, dung, guts, and blood,*
> *Drown'd puppies, shaking sprats, all drenched in mud,*
> *Dead cats, and turnip tops, come tumbling down the flood.*

Clearly a road was needed here more than a waterway, and in 1733 the canal down to Fleet Bridge was arched over, the wharves became roads, and a covered market was built on the central strip. The Fleet scheme was a success in the end, but, as so often happens in the planning of towns, not in the way its progenitors had first intended. Today the Fleet still runs below ground and serves as a large sewer below Farringdon Street and New Bridge Street.

Although the schemes of the Quay and the Fleet were largely failures, the legislation on new methods of building houses produced a general architectural effect throughout the City that was fully successful. The Rebuilding Acts provided the City with an admirable new building code that gave birth to a fresh, coherent and truly urban style. All new houses had to be of brick or stone and separated by solid party walls, such being 'not only more comely and durable, but also more safe against future perils of fire'. The finest houses would be erected along the important highways and those less imposing along the minor streets. For the sake of 'better regulation, uniformity and gracefulness', only four types of houses were to be allowed: two, three and four storeys high excluding basements and roof garrets, and a special fourth type of four storeys 'of the greatest bigness' belonging to the wealthiest merchants which did not have to be aligned along the street but could be set back. This ruling was very rigid and in the rebuilding many compromises were, in fact, made.

The grand mansions of the fourth type, mostly built near the Guildhall, were enthusiastically described some forty years after the Fire in Hutton's *New View of London* (1708) as being 'magnificent with courts, offices and all other necessary apartments inclosed to themselves, and noble gates and frontispieces towards the streets, richly furnished within'.

On the four-storey type, part of the regulations read: 'And for the greater grace and uniformity of the buildings in the high and principal streets, it is enacted, that all houses hereafter to be erected in any of them shall have balconies four foot broad with rails and bars of iron, equally distant from the ground. Every of which balconies shall contain in length two parts of the front of the house on which it shall be placed, in three parts to be divided; and the remaining vacancy of the front shall be supplied with a pent-house of the breadth of the balcony, to be covered with lead, slate, or tile, and to be sealed with plastering underneath. And that the water-falling, as well from the tops of the said houses, as from the said balconies and pent-houses, be conveyed into the channels, by party pipes on the sides or fronts of the said houses. And that pavements under every of the said balconies and pent-houses, be made of good and sufficient broad flat stone, at the charge of the builder.'

The lesser houses of two and three storeys were plain, though comely enough, with enrichments concentrated on classical doorways and ornamental eaves. Windows were everywhere tall, wide casements (soon to be superseded by the so-called Georgian sash), and walls were of red hand-made bricks

51. *The Royal Exchange as rebuilt to the arcaded and ebullient design of Edward Jerman. It was burned down in 1838.*

broken by projecting bands at each storey. In all cases rain was conveyed from the roofs into gutters and then down pipes to channels in the streets.

In constructing the new houses builders had to conform, on pain of heavy penalties for default, including imprisonment, to certain standards: thickness of brick walls, heights between floors and ceilings, depths of cellars, sizes of floor and roof scantlings, and adequate distances between fireplaces and timbers. Jerry building was out. The result was that the houses produced by the Rebuilding Acts were excellent in their orderly, unpretentious and solid way, and they came deeply to affect domestic design throughout the country.

Building of houses was sporadic and piecemeal, and some years were to pass before whole streets were completely built up with contiguous dwellings. At the start many of the houses were rented to alehouse keepers and victuallers to serve the hordes of artisans employed in rebuilding. Samuel Rolle in *London's Resurrection*, published in 1668, estimated that at that time some eight hundred

52. *The rebuilt Goldsmiths' Hall in 1691. The plan is on page 82.*

houses had been built. From them the outlook was depressing. 'Methinks', wrote the divine, 'it is an ill prospect, and a ghastly sight, for those that look from the balconies or tops of their stately new houses, to see ashes and ruinous heaps on every side of them – to see ten private houses (besides churches and public halls) in the dust for one that is raised again'. In the main streets like Cheapside merchants had built their new dwellings but would not live there 'till the neighbourhood be increased, fearing thieves as well as unprofitable trade'. But then barely two years had passed since the Fire. After that, rebuilding began to gain momentum so that by the summer of 1669 the number of houses, some still under scaffolding, amounted to about sixteen hundred, and, although house building slackened the next year, when many workmen were diverted to start the public buildings and churches, by 1672 many streets had been continuously built up with an occasional break of green where a church had stood in its yard.

Strangely enough, a great number of new houses stood empty for some time. An official return of February 1673 gave the number of uninhabited houses in the City as 3,423 with 961 remaining to be built. As a result property prices fell alarmingly. One trouble was that many traders had spent all they possessed on rebuilding and could not afford to lay in new stocks; another was that some had moved to other towns or to the suburbs and the Strand, were prospering, and saw no reason to return to the City where restrictions were firmer and liabilities higher. Some wealthy men had moved west into the fashionable world, while the poor could not afford to live in the new brick houses. There was also a trade recession which reduced business incentives and the desire to achieve 'freedom' of the City for which a high fee, or some favour, was demanded before a man could trade within the Wall. The Corporation tried to remedy the situation by ordering all aldermen to return with their families to the City under threats of heavy penalties if they failed to do so, and, for encouragement, those who took up residence would be allowed freedom of the City gratis.

Then trade began to revive and before long the City, now far healthier and more commodious, functional and seemly as a great centre of commerce than the pre-Fire capital had been, was bustling once more with all its nine thousand new houses, great and small, fully inhabited.

How long, in fact, did the entire rebuilding of the City take? On the south side of the Fire Monument was inscribed: 'London rises again, whether with greater speed or greater magnificence is doubtful, three short years complete that which was considered the work of an age'. It was an absurd boast as the facts show, facts that were known when the words were cut. Evelyn saw the truth three years after the Fire when the City 'now began a little to revive after its sad calamity'.

Four years after the Fire new buildings covered only about a half of the devastated area; none of Wren's churches were yet under construction and the foundation stone of the new St Paul's had not been laid. Such public buildings as the Guildhall, Royal Exchange and Custom House were not finished, and most Companies were still without their Halls; the Companies, indeed, were not fully accommodated until 1685. All Wren's fifty-one parish churches were more or less complete before the end of the century but even then the steeples of a few were not finished until well into the eighteenth century – that is about fifty years after the Fire. The great cathedral was whole, at least nominally, in 1708 when Wren was seventy-eight and when, in his presence, his son laid the highest stone of the lantern above the cupola.

For two decades after the Fire many sites lay empty all over the area, decorated, as were many of the bombed sites for so long after the Second World War, with wild flowers, notably with *Sisymbrium irio*, known demotically ever since the Fire as London Rocket. Although most sites had been built over within ten years of the Fire, the last plot was not staked by the surveyors until 1696. The entire work, when Wren's fabulous skyline could be seen complete across the river, thus took about forty-five years to accomplish. This

53, 54. *Two old engravings show men quarrying stone and making bricks at the time the City was rebuilding.*

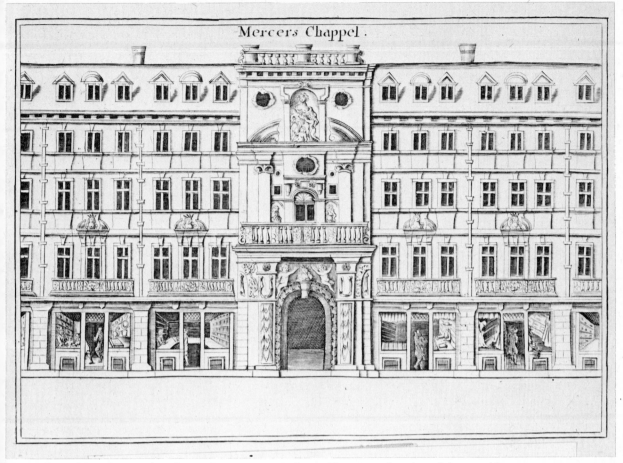

55. *The Mercers' Chapel in 1681 set in a typical post-Fire street elevation of shops and large houses.*

was not bad going when all the difficulties are considered. It was an enormous job, undertaken at a time when construction depended on small builders and handicrafts without the help of mass-produced parts, rationalization of methods, mechanical equipment, railways, petrol engines or telephones.

Two big questions had demanded replies from the citizens faced with the rebuilding: the first, inevitably, was 'Where was the money to come from?' the second 'How could enough craftsmen and materials be obtained?'

The first Rebuilding Act called for a tax on coal entering the City of one shilling a ton, the first proceeds of which would cover compensation for land acquired for street widening, for restoring river wharves and rebuilding the City prisons. In the second Act the tax was increased to three shillings a ton, and was eventually to pay not only for street improvements, wharves, quays, prisons and markets but also largely for Wren's new churches and cathedral, although private donations did help the church building. The tax was to survive

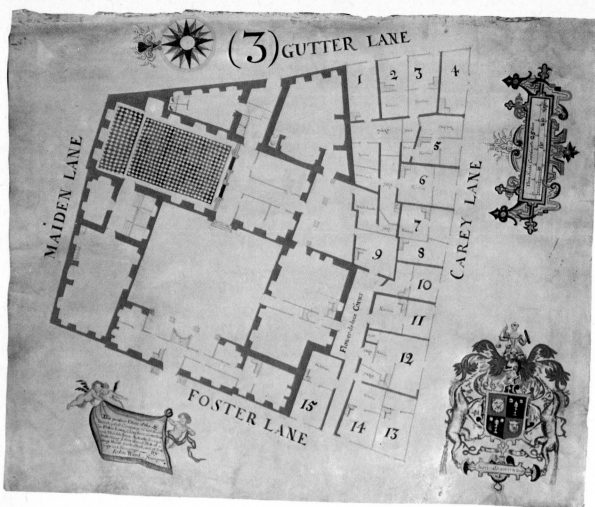

56. *A plan of Goldsmiths' Hall in 1691. A general view is on page 78.*

for two hundred years to provide lucre that, if not utterly filthy, certainly made for ubiquitous soot and frequent fogs in the metropolis.

The rebuilding of the Guildhall, seat of City government, and of the Sessions House of the Old Bailey were financed by fines imposed on those who wished to avoid the office of alderman. The Corporation also borrowed large sums of money, even though modern methods of monopolistic credit creation were not yet fully developed; the Bank of England, a private concern that was to have 'benefit of interest on all monies which it creates out of nothing' in the words of one of its founders, William Paterson, was not established until 1694. Presumably the goldsmiths in the Lombardy tradition had their usurious methods of issuing loans based on receipts for gold objects which did not exist.

Gold coins, as Pepys knew well, were the safest form of saving, and rich men hoarded their coins in bags under their own roofs, for paper money, in its modern form at least did not exist.

The City Companies had to find their own means for rebuilding their Halls in face of the Fire losses and the loans they had been forced to make to the Commonwealth and then to the king. Some raised the wind by selling houses they owned, and by renting their Halls. They also offered each other mutual aid by sharing Halls for a time.

57. Sisymbrium irio *or London Rocket, the wild flower that flourished on the unoccupied sites of the post-Fire City, as it did later on the bombed sites after the Second World War.*

The State financed the Crown properties from its own revenue, as in the case of the Custom House, and no doubt many wealthy merchants used their hoards of gold either to finance their own projects or as interest-bearing loans. But the full facts of how the rebuilding of the City was financed are far from clear. Presumably private savings, mostly in stocking hoards belonging to those who had not been ruined by the Fire and who were not drooping in the debtors' prisons of Ludgate, the Fleet and Marshalsea, paid for most of the new private houses. No public assistance or building society loans were available to help the individual house builder, although some encouragement was given by the king when he remitted the Hearth Tax, and when a tenant rebuilt, ground rent was in many cases waived for a number of years by the freeholder.

The trade guilds in the City at the time of the Fire were less powerful than they had been in medieval times but they were still autocratic enough, and the freemen of the crafts monopolized all building work in the City. This put the City fathers in a quandary, but not for long because the solution was patent. Either London had to be rapidly rebuilt or lose its trade and its wealth. The issue was decided by the Rebuilding Act in the following terms: 'All carpenters, bricklayers, masons, plasterers, joiners, and other artificers, workmen and labourers to be employed in the said buildings, who are not freemen of the said City shall for the space of seven years next ensuing, and for so long time after as until the said buildings shall be fully finished, have and enjoy such and the same liberty of working, and being set to work in the said building, as the freemen of the City of the same trades and professions have and ought to enjoy; any usage or custom of the City to the contrary notwithstanding. And that such artificers as aforesaid, which for the space of seven years shall have wrought in the rebuilding of the City in their respective arts, shall from and after the said seven years have and enjoy the same liberty to work as freemen of the said City for and during their natural lives.'

The result was that building craftsmen flocked to the City from all over the country. Their wages were fixed by two judges of the King's Bench, strikes were declared illegal, and anyone withholding labour would be imprisoned for a month or heavily fined. The judges were empowered to fix the prices of materials if the need should arise, and, in order that building materials might be in adequate supply, the restraints imposed by the Navigation Acts were removed to allow the free import of timber, bricks and tiles from abroad. At Whitechapel and other suburbs a large new industry arose in brickmaking. Even so materials were not always readily to hand, least of all timber, while stone from Portland, much needed for the king's own enterprises and for the City's new monumental buildings, was rationed.

But in the end the job was done, and considering all the difficulties it was remarkably well done.

6. Fifty-one New Churches

To what extent was Wren, as chief architect, personally responsible for the designing of the new City and its buildings? It is not easy to give a clear answer. He certainly helped to frame the two Rebuilding Acts, the rejected master plan was undoubtedly his, and so was the cathedral (with a few minor exceptions of detail), but of the fifty-one new parish churches not all, as we have seen, may have been built entirely according to his design, although he no doubt signed his approval of them all and certainly himself designed the outstanding examples. In planning he was directly concerned with the riverside quay and the Fleet Canal, the widening of King Street and Queen Street and the spaces around Guildhall, but the general lay-out and adjustment of streets, alleys, and plots for the new houses were left to Robert Hooke.

With the more important buildings and houses, apart from the churches and cathedral, Wren was only sometimes directly concerned. He could not do everything himself and, being a wise man, no doubt decided at an early stage to delegate certain functions to others and concentrate his own creative energies on the limited but important sphere of the main churches and cathedral, a sphere which gave his genius ample scope and, as a devout member of the Church of England, son of a parson, nephew of a bishop and reared in the Protestant tradition, also offered him personal satisfaction and solace in an exacting position of responsibility. No evidence exists that he designed any of the Halls of the City Companies. Some were designed by Edward Jerman, who also designed the grand, arcaded, and somewhat mannerist Royal Exchange which stood until 1838 when it perished in a fire. The most notable public buildings with which Wren was certainly closely involved were the Custom House, the Guildhall and the new Temple Bar.

At the Guildhall, Wren raised the great hall by twenty feet, provided a roof and gallery and designed anew the surrounding buildings of Council Chamber, Parlour, Town Clerk's Office, Mayor's Court and others. There the work went on without interruption until the end of 1675, and even then the temporary flat roof Wren had provided had not been replaced; indeed, it remained for two centuries until the existing high-pitched, trussed timber roof in medieval style was constructed in 1866.

Temple Bar across Fleet Street, where it provided a monumental entrance gate to the City on the west, was completed in 1672 and is probably wholly Wren's work. A triumphal arch based on precedents from antique Rome, at least as an idea if not in design, it was taken down in 1878 and re-erected at Theobalds Park in Hertfordshire, where it can still be seen.

Wren may also have designed the Deanery of St Paul's, the College of Arms

58. *A painting of Wren's Temple Bar from the west shows a typical scene in the rebuilt City c. 1760.*

and, with help from Hooke, the new Navy Office in Seething Lane which was burned down in 1673 almost as soon as it was built. The Fire Monument, described in the last chapter, seems to have been more the creation of Hooke than of Wren. So far as is known Wren himself designed none of the new houses. He was never dictatorial and always encouraged the creative expression of his subordinates and partners.

Wren's chief contributions were the cathedral and the churches that, with their variety of towers and steeples, gave the new City its unique character and its splendid skyline. Although the parish churches were of far greater importance in daily life than they are now, not only as places of worship but as centres of local Christian communities, possessing summoning bells that had to ring loud enough to be heard clearly at least as far as the parish boundaries, it was not until 1670, the year of the additional Rebuilding Act that any of Wren's churches were begun. That year fourteen of them were started, each design quite different from any other and displaying the master's hand: St Christopher-le-Stocks, St Lawrence Jewry, St Bride, St Michael Cornhill, St Mary-le-Bow, St Dionis Backchurch, St Benet Fink, St Michael Wood Street, St Mary Aldermanbury, St Vedast Foster Lane, St Mary-le-Hill, St Edmund King and Martyr, St Mildred Poultry, St Olave Jewry. But some time had still to pass before bells were installed in their towers, and, as the City grew, for many years no joyful peals nor doleful knells, no bells answering Sunday bells, drowned the customary noises of the town.

According to the chronicler Fabyan, the City in 1516 contained no less than one hundred and thirteen parish churches, but at the time of the Fire there were fewer – ninety-seven within the Wall and ten in the surrounding Liberties. As we have seen, eighty-seven were destroyed in the Fire either wholly or in part, and only twenty-two survived, eight of which are still in being, three having been damaged in the Second World War and afterwards restored. They are St Olave Hart Street, All Hallows Barking, St Katherine Cree and St Andrew Undershaft (both in Leadenhall Street), St Helen Bishopsgate, St Ethelburga Bishopsgate, St Giles Cripplegate (Victorianized), St Bartholomew the Great West Smithfield (Norman and London's oldest).

While rebuilding was in progress, how were parishioners served? A Commission of 1670 consisting of the Archbishop of Canterbury, the Bishop of London and the Lord Mayor decided to raise temporary tabernacles at convenient places in the City on the sites of old churches or on graveyards. The finance came from the increased coal dues, the average cost of each being a hundred and fifty pounds. Eventually thirty, simply constructed of timber on brick bases, were erected and served their purpose well enough – precursors of the Tin Tabernacles of Victorian times.

The City discouraged too rapid a rebuilding of the churches because, for one thing, stone was in limited supply, even if some of the stone from the old structures could be used. By far the largest quantity of new stone came in a regular fleet of small coasters from Portland, where even if the stone was in ample supply, the labour for quarrying it and the means of transporting it were not. Yet by January 1678 the first fourteen churches were nearly complete and five others well advanced. By 1683 twenty-five were in full use and seventeen more nearly finished, but not until 1721 was the last of the fifty-one new churches opened for worship.

For building the City churches Wren was paid about £100 a year; he received the same sum for repairing Westminster Abbey, but for the cathedral he received £200 a year – by no means large sums even at that time. Yet there

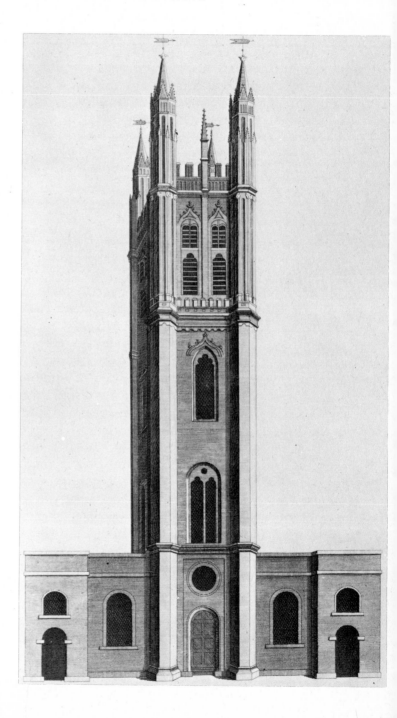

59, 60. *Left, Wren's own drawing of his finest steeple – that of St Mary-le-Bow in Cheapside. Right, a print of St Michael Cornhill from the west with its classical body by Wren to which Hawksmoor added a Gothic tower.*

were perks the acceptance of which did not in those days bring disrepute. Parishioners were often impatient at the delays in the rebuilding of their particular church, and bribes were often offered to Wren to hasten the work – sometimes a good dinner, at other times an emolument of twenty guineas in a silk purse or the presentation to his lady of a pair of silver candlesticks. At the completion of a work he might be offered a gift of gratitude, as in the case of St Magnus where in 1681 a hogshead of claret was ordered for presentation to the architect. It is obvious, however, that Wren never became a rich man.

The two main traits of the City churches are, firstly, the ingenuity of their planning often on restricted, irregular and hemmed-in sites in a manner that would satisfy the requirements of the Church of England rituals with as much openness as possible and a minimum of supporting columns in the interior so that all could see the preacher and hear his sermons as clearly as possible; secondly, their embellishment with bell-towers and steeples of astonishing diversity and virtuosity which, since the air was not restricted like the sites, could rise as high as wished and be freely decorated.

The churches were, in fact, planned for the Anglican liturgy of sermon, scripture reading and celebration of Communion at the altar. As a Commissioner of the 1708 Act for fifty new churches, Wren was to comment that parish churches should be as large as possible but should not, in the reformed religion, be larger 'than that all who are present can both hear and see'. The Romanists, he pointed out, may build larger churches since 'it is enough if they hear the murmur of the Mass, and see the Elevation of the Host, but ours are to be fitted for Auditories'. Wren stated his aims in the designing of the City churches in this way: 'To bring them out as far as possible from the obscure lanes, not too nicely to observe east and west, unless they fall out properly; such fronts as shall lie most open in view should be adorned with porticos, both for beauty and convenience, which, together with handsome spires, or lanterns, rising in good proportion above the neighbouring houses . . . may be a sufficient ornament to the town without a great expense, for enriching the outward walls of the churches, in which plainness and duration ought principally, if not wholly, to be studied'. On towers he wrote with typical practicality: 'When a parish is divided, I suppose it may be thought sufficient if the mother church has a tower, large enough for a good ring of bells, and the other churches, smaller towers for two or three bells; because great towers and lofty steeples are sometimes more than half the charge of the church.'

Wren's steeples and towers can be divided into three groups: (i) nine stone steeples, (ii) twelve square towers, (iii) nineteen lead-covered timber spires and lanterns. In many cases the towers were built in two stages: first, the square tower itself which could, if necessary, stand on its own as an entity, and then, if and when funds became available, the ornate steeple could be added above it.

The churches varied greatly in quality, richness, and interest of design. Some were merely small, unassuming boxes, others mediocre, a few splendid. Detailing is sometimes crude compared with that of St Paul's, and it is clear that Wren did not always supervise it personally but left it to his subordinates or, more often, to individual craftsmen. As he noted in one case 'the order is the workmen's invention'. Occasionally Wren could enjoy a broad and unrestricted site as at St Lawrence Jewry, the Corporation's own church by the Guildhall, but even here the outer face of the pilastered east wall, unusually elaborate as it is, had to be set slightly askew and is not parallel with the inner face of the wall, which is therefore thicker at the south end where the windows were given arches in false perspective as compensation. Few of the churches had more than a shallow recess at the east end and many had a carved oak reredos there, while fittings and furnishings, and sometimes elaborate projecting clocks like those at St Edmund the King in Lombard Street and at St Magnus Martyr by London Bridge, were provided not by the Coal Tax but by private gifts or parish funds. Wren often supervised such furnishings, which were executed with much elaborate, if sometimes rough, craftsmanship. Plaster decoration tended to be crude but the reredos and the carved pulpits with sounding boards above were often superb examples of fanciful carvings of classical orders, flowers, wreaths and cupids. Interior walls were painted white or stone-colour with some gilding here and there, but stained glass was rarely used because this not only reduced cost but made as full a use of available light as possible on sites that were often darkly hemmed in. Tall, ornate sword rests of wrought iron were a common feature of the interiors, and a number of these have survived.

Plans varied in type, some nearly square as at St Mary-le-Bow with its four internal columns, some aisled and perhaps galleried, some with intersecting barrel vaults to form Greek Cross plans, some polygonal and domed, some oval. Ceilings could be domed, vaulted, groined or flat (as at St Lawrence Jewry). The main material was Portland stone, but sometimes red brick was used for the walling as at St Benet Paul's Wharf.

Whether or not the churches can be termed baroque is a moot point, for Wren in his calm, mathematical manner was only partly a baroque designer, unlike his pupil Hawksmoor, or Vanbrugh and Archer who were uncompromisingly so in a theatrical, emotional style. The cathedral is obviously baroque in many ways but the churches have few features that can be termed baroque in the full, ebullient sense of the word. A few of the steeples were, in fact, Gothic in style and many others were derived from Dutch and Scandinavian examples. Their general character, though ultimately stemming from Vitruvius and Serlio in a Roman way, is original, inventive and personal. Three of Wren's steeples were pure Gothic pastiche – at St Alban Wood Street,

61. *Wren's finest church interior – that of St Stephen Walbrook near Mansion House, as depicted by Malton in 1792.*

62. *St Magnus Martyr Church and old London Bridge c. 1810. The houses on the old bridge were removed c. 1762, and the east pavement was directed under the tower of this church.*

at St Dunstan-in-the-East (based on the pre-Fire St Mary-le-Bow) and at St
Mary's Aldermary where Wren was compelled to design the whole church in
Gothic style (with pleasing fan vaulting of plaster) because a large donor
stipulated that the new church should be a copy of the old one. Yet even
Wren's Gothic departures reveal him as an unromantic Latinist.

Many Wren churches were destroyed or severely damaged by the bombs of
the Second World War, but many had vanished before then in the nineteenth
and early twentieth centuries, mostly in the overbearing interests of commerce.
St Antholin Budge Row and St Benet Fink, for example, were demolished in
the 1840s; St Christopher-le-Stocks was destroyed even earlier – in 1781 as a
result of the Gordon riots. All Hallows Lombard Street was demolished in
1939 and its fine woodwork, monuments and tower were re-erected somewhat uneasily at the new church of All Hallows at Twickenham, while St
Mary Aldermanbury has been rebuilt at Fulton, Missouri, as a symbol of
Anglo-American concord. A few towers without the bodies of the churches
remain and a few have been rebuilt since the war in more or less their original

63. *St Bride's, Fleet Street, looking east with St Paul's in the distance as revealed in a print
of 1753.*

64. *St Lawrence Jewry and the Guildhall as painted by Malton c. 1790.*

forms. A number were debased in Victorian times, like St Michael Cornhill, with its porch by Giles Gilbert Scott.

In spite of losses and degradations much of Wren's work in the City has survived. The total number of old City churches still standing is thirty-nine of which twenty-five are Wren's, apart from such Wren relics as the tower of St Mary Somerset in Upper Thames Street with its remarkable crown of urns and obelisks. To save and use as many as possible of the old City churches after the war, the City of London (Guild Churches) Act was passed in 1952 to free some of the churches from parochial responsibilities so that now, under the title of Guild Churches, they serve only week-day congregations and carry out special kinds of religious work. St Stephen Walbrook, for instance, is the centre of the Samaritans. As the former Bishop of London, Dr Wand, stated, the Act would turn the City into 'a great laboratory in which new methods of ministry, new spiritual expedients and new pastoral techniques may be tried out for the benefit of the Church as a whole . . . such as religious drama, Christian films, visual aids in religious education, apologetics, religious art and literature'. Even for the agnostic and the atheist of civilized inclinations, this was an admirable notion, for it has saved many a fine old church from decay and demolition. Now most of the churches are open at midday during the week but are closed at week-ends.

For full descriptions of the Wren churches the reader must turn to works such as Gerald Cobb's *The Old Churches of London* and, as a guide to surviving examples, his *London City Churches*, an admirable brochure published by the City Corporation. A work of particular value is John Clayton's folio of 1849 which contains measured drawings of all the City churches made before so many were destroyed. Something of interest can be found in all the surviving churches, but only a few selected cases can be noticed here. St Magnus Martyr, for instance, in Lower Thames Street, is a fine church, in spite of being so over-whelmed, insulted, and darkened by the neighbouring office block of Adelaide House. When the houses on old London Bridge were removed it could have been seen at its best with the footway of the bridge running below its western tower, but even now the internal walls still hold, in T. S. Eliot's famous London poem, that 'inexplicable splendour of Ionian white and gold'. (Ghost hunters may like to know that it is London's only haunted church.)

St Martin's Ludgate must be mentioned for its beautiful steeple of lead with its ogee-domed base, its projecting balcony below the lantern and its slender obelisk terminating in a ball. Here Wren, undoubtedly with the general townscape in mind, made the spire serve as a perfect introductory foil to the great western towers and swelling dome of St Paul's at the top of the hill.

St Margaret Lothbury, behind the Bank of England, is notable for its carved wood furnishings, including the remarkable entwining double-helixes of the screen columns. Here too is a marble font with sides bearing bas-reliefs of biblical subjects attributed to Grinling Gibbons. This is the least altered of all the Wren churches.

But the five most outstanding of the surviving churches are St Mary-le-Bow Cheapside, St Bride Fleet Street, St Lawrence Jewry by the Guildhall, St Benet Paul's Wharf in Thames Street, and St Stephen Walbrook near the Mansion House.

St Mary-le-Bow has a strange plan dictated by the site; only the tower, brought forward by Wren to the street line, fronts Cheapside. There entrance

65. *Looking east down Cheapside as rebuilt after the Fire with the tower and spire of St Mary-le-Bow on the south side.*

to the church is made through a grand portico, thence through a lobby under the tower and into the body of the church where a turn to the left is needed to face the altar. Burnt out in 1941 and partly rebuilt, the interior with its arched roof is wide with three bays, the nave and aisles separated by piers with half-columns in front, an arrangement, according to *Parentalia*, derived from the Basilica Maxentius, the Temple of Peace, in Rome. The interior is not particularly thrilling; the glory of the building is the elaborate steeple of Portland stone. Completed in the 1680s, as the first of its classical kind in England, the base of the tower is founded on a Roman causeway lying eighteen feet below street level and its spire soars up to two hundred and twenty-five feet. It holds reminders of the tower of the old fifteenth-century church which stood further south with its corona of pinnacles and bows of flying buttresses.

On the north side of the basic square tower facing Cheapside is one of Wren's few monumental church entrances consisting of a pair of Doric columns supporting an entablature on which are seated two boys or cherubim on either side of an oval window, the whole set in a rusticated niche. Above this the tower walls continue uninterrupted until they reach the belfry which is articulated by round-headed windows on each face and Ionic pilasters at the corners. Then comes a balustrade with corner scrolls bearing urns which gently introduce the circular structure of the steeple above – first a round colonnade like a temple followed by a kind of open dome composed of twelve flying buttresses supporting a smaller and square temple; then more urns and finally an obelisk topped by a ball and a vane, about eight feet across in the form of a dragon. A sectional drawing shows the steeple to have a complex construction with a cylindrical core containing a spiral staircase of wood. This is Wren's triumphant masterpiece and may be regarded as the finest Renaissance steeple not only in England but in the whole of Europe.

St Bride Fleet Street has Wren's second finest steeple, in spite of having lost three feet from its top when struck by lightning in 1764. Henley called it a madrigal in stone. Though less elaborate than that of St Mary-le-Bow it has subtlety and charm. Again the base is square with a belfry having corner pilasters supporting segmental pediments and large arched openings on each face. The steeple above is stepped back in four octagonal stages, each with pilasters standing on pedestals and topped by an octagonal obelisk. The whole looks, indeed, rather like the spire above the dome of the unexecuted Warrant Design for St Paul's. The pilasters diminish in height at each stage but the pedestals increase in height, so providing a feeling of soaring lightness as well as of strength. Between the pilasters on each storey are round-headed openings, and within the steeple runs a staircase lit by the openings on whose sills pigeons nest and croon.

Known as the cathedral of Fleet Street, St Bride's is the church of printers, journalists and writers. Living within short walking distance of the church at the time of the Fire were many men of literary renown such as Dryden, Milton, Izaak Walton, Lovelace, Aubrey, Thomas Spratt and Samuel Pepys who was christened there. Later, when Wren's edifice was standing, the area was associated with names such as Samuel Johnson, Boswell, Garrick, Reynolds, Goldsmith, Burke, Addison, Pope, Hogarth, Mrs Siddons and Samuel Richardson, father of the English novel. Later still the district was well known to such distinguished figures as Charles Lamb, Wordsworth, Keats, Leigh Hunt and Hazlitt.

St Bride's was one of the first post-Fire churches to be completed and it was among the largest and most costly. It rests on ancient foundations, the earliest being Roman, conceivably those of an early Christian church set outside the Roman wall. Seven churches seem to have stood here at different periods. Wren's fine design was gutted in the fire raid of 29 December 1940, but it has been rebuilt more or less according to the original, although the galleries have not been replaced. The arcades of coupled columns have been re-erected, carrying a barrel vault over the nave and cross vaults over the aisles, but the east end is now different with a freestanding reredos covering the window, around which is painted a clever *trompe l'oeil* by Glyn Jones giving the impression of a semi-circular apse, its subject based on a description of the original fresco in Hatton's *New View of London* of 1708. The old organ has gone from the west end and there now stand two large figures of St Paul and St Bridgit by David McFall. An error of judgement in the rebuilding was the erection of carved screens and stalls where they hide the lower part of the columns.

During excavations made when the church was being rebuilt after the war, relics were revealed of a thousand years of London's history, and the crypt now contains a fascinating museum of that history, including the Roman remains.

St Lawrence Jewry is also one of Wren's larger churches and, being free-standing as few others are, its outer east wall is elaborately detailed with exceptional care with four Corinthian columns, their capitals linked by carved swags and supporting a pediment and five arched windows. 'A very fine church' according to Pepys, and so it should be as the Corporation's own, and standing, as it does, on the approach to the Guildhall. The word Jewry refers to the Jews who lived in this area from the reign of William the Conqueror until their banishment by Edward I. St Lawrence was the martyr who in 258 during the Valerian persecutions was ordered to deliver the church's treasures and fulfilled the ruling by producing all the sick and the poor he could muster while secretly dispersing the valuables. He was consequently flayed alive and then roasted on a gridiron, emblems of which decorated the church.

Wren's original building was opened in 1677 at a service attended by Charles II. Like St Bride's, it was gutted in the fire raid of 1940, except for the tower and walls, but it has been well rebuilt according to the original at considerable cost. A stained-glass window in the vestibule offers a tribute in depicting the figure of Wren flanked by his Master Carver and Master Mason with the modern reconstruction shown below. The tower and spire are copies of the originals, including the weather-vane in the form of a gridiron, though the shaft of the vane now takes the shape of an incendiary bomb. A ring of eight bells has been re-installed, while the original painting of St Lawrence in martyrdom, which was saved in the Blitz, now hangs in the vestry.

Unhappily the superb wood carvings and other details which graced the original perished in 1940. These were of the finest and the pride of the parish, notably a gallery supported by Corinthian columns and carrying an organ embellished with cartouches of musical instruments, also rich door-cases with swags and broken pediments, and a vestry more lavishly furbished than any similar room of the period that loved rich decorations, with a ceiling painted by the younger Fuller of figures flying into the mystery of the infinite azure.

St Benet Paul's Wharf in Lower Thames Street is very different from St Lawrence Jewry. It is homely and not very large, but it has great charm. Happily it was among the few Wren churches to escape serious damage in the

66. *Looking south at the Stocks Market in 1738 where the Mansion House was to be built in 1753. The dome and tower of Wren's St Stephen Walbrook is in the background.*

war. Possibly Hooke had a hand in its design for its walls are of a rich red brick patterned with burnt headers and having stone quoins and carved stone garlands over the round-headed windows, all revealing a Dutch influence: its source may be Philip Vingboon's book which Hooke acquired in 1674, three years before the church was begun. The tower is of stone and brick and carries a small lead cupola with a lantern above. The whole is endearing and the three hipped roofs on the north side add to the picturesque effect. The site was a difficult one on account of the steep slope which renders the south side ten feet higher than the north. Inside is a nave with a single aisle. The building is now occupied by the Church of Wales and, at the time of writing when Thames Street and neighbourhood are undergoing reconstruction, it can be seen in

67. *The tower of St Stephen Walbrook surrounded by post-Fire houses as revealed in 1811 by T.H. Shepherd.*

isolation from Queen Victoria Street with the backdrop of the river and south bank behind it.

Lastly we come to Wren's most accomplished church interior – that of St Stephen Walbrook, near the Mansion House. 'Never was so sweet a kernel in so rough a shell' declares Bumpus in his *Ancient London Churches*. 'The tameness of its form, a simple cell enclosed by four walls, wholly disappears behind the unique and varied arrangement of its sixteen Corinthian columns.' Wren did in fact, design a splendid portico for the north side, drawings of which have been found, but it was never built. The interior has justly received more praise than any other, and it is of particular interest in having structural links in its small way with Wren's great cathedral – a miniature solution of the difficult problem with which Wren wrestled for some time of combining nave, aisles and transepts with a domed space. It was a problem Wren never solved with full satisfaction at St Paul's.

Through engravings, the interior achieved international renown during the eighteenth century. As *A Critical Review of Public Buildings in London* published in 1734 declared: 'Walbrook Church, so little known among us,

is famous all over Europe, and is justly reputed the master-piece of the celebrated Sir Christopher Wren. Perhaps Italy itself can produce no modern
building that can vie with this, in taste and proportion . . . Foreigners very
justly call our judgment in question for understanding its grace no better,
and allowing it no higher a degree of fame.' The parish was lucky in being
patronized by the Grocer's Company so that money and enthusiastic patronage
were available to create a rare structure.

The structure is hard to describe in words, though it is clear enough on sight
and even in drawings and photographs. The dome of timber and plaster,
decorated with embossed panels and supporting a lantern, rests not on the
outer walls but on eight equal arches with intermediate pendentives supported
by eight Corinthian columns without fluting standing on tall pedestals. At
the four corners the entablatures of the orders return to form right angles
supported there by columns with groined vaults above, thus allowing the
inclusion of two additional windows at each corner to increase the light. At
the east end is a short recess covered by a vault with a large end window and
two smaller side windows, while to the north and south of the domed space
are short barrel-vaulted recesses ending in large windows. To the west four
more columns like the rest support a flat ceiling over a short nave.

The church was only partly damaged in the war and the rich furnishings
were luckily saved. A loss is the replacement with low benches of the original
high pews reaching the height of the pedestals on which the columns stand.
They formed an important part of Wren's conception and should surely be
reinstated in modern form in order to complete this fine interior. Sir John
Vanbrugh lies buried in this church.

In 1708, the ninth year of Queen Anne's reign, an Act of Parliament was
passed for the erection of fifty new churches at Westminster and in the City
suburbs which were required to serve the ever-expanding metropolis. Although in his seventy-sixth year, Wren was appointed one of the commissioners. The number of new churches built never reached fifty and Wren
designed none of them, which was a pity because here at least all the sites were
open and unrestricted and would have allowed him ample scope. Outstanding
examples of the new churches are that upturned footstool, Thomas Archer's
St John the Evangelist in Smith Square, Westminster, Nicholas Hawksmoor's
Christ Church, Spitalfields, his St Anne's, Limehouse, and his St George's-in-
the-East, all strongly baroque, as well as James Gibbs' delightful St Mary-le-
Strand and his St Martin-in-the-Fields at the corner of Trafalgar Square, both
more classical and Wren-like than the others. Gibbs came directly under the
influence of Wren when he returned from Rome in 1709 and through his
Book of Architecture of 1728 the Wren steeple and basilica plan with its aisles
and side galleries above spread to the new towns of the American colonies.

7. New Cathedral

The first stone of the new basilica was not laid until 1675, nine years after the Fire. Delays were caused first by a misguided idea that the calcined ruins of the old cathedral could be rehabilitated, and then by Wren's designing of a number of successive schemes which proved unacceptable.

With his superior knowledge and good sense, Wren knew quite well that nothing could be done with the old building and repeatedly advised that tinkering with the riven walls would be futile. Yet for two years the church authorities ignored his advice. Meanwhile Wren had fitted up a temporary choir and auditory at the west end of the desolation behind Inigo Jones's grand portico, while a half-hearted repair of the ancient fabric was being attempted against Wren's protests.

Then, in 1668, Dean Sancroft summoned Wren hurriedly to London in a letter which read: 'What you whispered in my ear at your last coming hither is now come to pass. Our work at the west-end of St Paul's is fallen about our ears. Your quick eye discerned the walls and pillars gone off their perpendiculars, and I believe other defects, too, which are now exposed to every common observer ... The third pillar from the west-end on the south-side, which

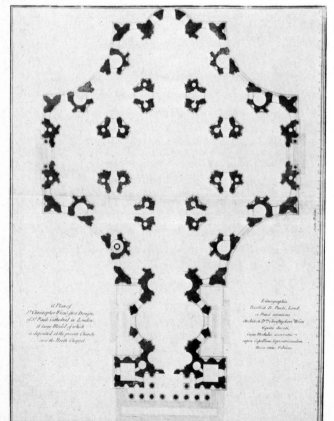

68. *The plan of the Great Model design for St Paul's Cathedral – Wren's favourite project with its large and small domes.*

69. *The Great Model, eighteen feet long, made in 1674 of oak and limewood.*

we had new encased with stone fell and carried scaffolds and all to the very ground. The second pillar . . . stands now alone with an enormous weight on the top of it; which we cannot hope should stand long, and yet we dare not venture to take it down . . . We most earnestly desire your presence and assistance with all possible speed.'

So the building had to be abandoned as a place of worship. Three months later Sancroft again wrote to Wren, this time on behalf of the Archbishop of Canterbury and the Bishops of London and Oxford, informing him that the resolution had been taken 'to frame a design, handsome and noble, and suitable to all the ends of it, and to the reputation of the City, and the nation, and to take it for granted, that money will be had to accomplish it'. In the end, as we have seen, most of the money came from the Coal Tax.

Wren sat at his drawing board and produced a design known as the First Model. This had a rectangular choir and a dome curiously placed at the west end like that of the mediaeval Temple church. The king approved it but others thought it not grand enough. So Wren prepared further designs, the first of which had a Greek Cross plan with a large dome above the crossing, and another which was a variant of it, called the Great Model. This had a large dome over the crossing and a smaller one at the west end with a west portico of eight Corinthian columns. An actual model of this was made in 1674 in oak and limewood eighteen feet long, now preserved in the Trophy Room of the Cathedral. It is a fine object revealing the lucid geometry of the concept with its main dome a hundred and twenty-five feet in diameter (eight feet wider than the final dome and only seventeen feet less than that of St Peter's, Rome) set on a drum pierced by round-headed windows – in the words of *Parentalia* 'something coloss [sic] and beautiful with a design antique and well studied'. The interior with eight bold piers supporting the drum and dome formed fascinating vistas of varying planes and spatial recessions that continually changed as one moved around.

This was Wren's favourite design and it is said that he wept when it was rejected, a tale that sounds apocryphal in view of his stoical and adaptable nature, but evidently he felt chagrin and frustration. The commissioners and clergy rejected it on the grounds that it was not large enough nor sufficiently 'cathedral fashion' in its plan, and perhaps they were alarmed by its unusual style based as it was on ideas that stemmed from papal Rome. Wren set to work again and produced his compromise Warrant Design with its Latin Cross plan that showed a continuity from the Middle Ages but with a general design in classical idiom. This was a practical improvement to the extent that a Latin Cross plan can be built in sections and then used in sections, whereas the Greek Cross building must be built as a whole before it can be used at all.

The Warrant Design, approved by Royal Warrant in 1675, was based to some extent on Jones's renewals of Old St Paul's, particularly in the porticos. It had a choir for daily services, a large nave for ceremonial occasions, and aisles for circulation, 'so ordered', as the Warrant declared, 'that it might be built and finished by parts'. A shallow dome rose above the crossing which supported a drum covered by a small dome and topped by a tall, slender wooden spire of six diminishing storeys like a pagoda, the whole rising almost as high as the spire at Salisbury. The single order on the façades of the Great Model was replaced by dual orders which were less impressive but necessary because it was discovered that the Portland quarries could not produce blocks for columns of more than four feet in diameter – a necessity that had to be accepted in the final design of St Paul's as we see it. The Warrant Design is somewhat bizarre and has never been much liked by the savants in spite of its merits.

Anyway, it was discarded, in spite of the Royal Warrant, and thereafter, *Parentalia* relates, Wren 'resolved to make no more models, or publicly expose his drawings, which (as he had found by experience) did but lose time and subjected his business many times to incompetent judges'. He had had enough of critical and indecisive committees and he knew he could always rely on the full confidence of the king.

And so 'by these means, at last, the scheme of the present mighty structure (different in some manner from the former, and preferable in his Majesty's own judgement, upon after-thoughts), was no sooner concluded on, and ordered by his Majesty, but begun and prosecuted by his surveyor, with vigour, in the year 1675. And the king was pleased to allow him the liberty in the prosecution of his work, to make some variations, rather ornamental than essential, as from time to time he should see proper; and to leave the whole to his own management.' During the thirty-five years of its building, Wren did constantly

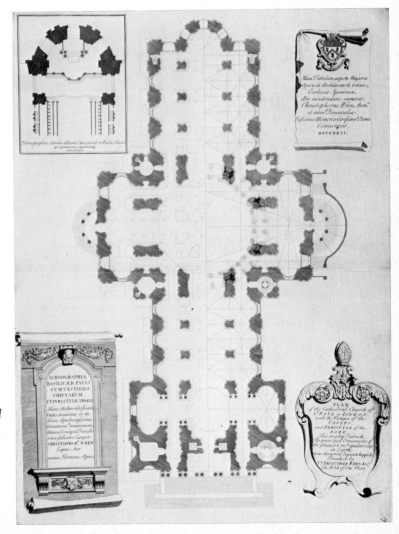

70. *The plan of the executed Cathedral engraved in 1726.*

71. *The horse ferry at Westminster early in the eighteenth century with a distant view of the rebuilt City. Lambeth Palace is on the right.*

modify his design, not least in the west-end towers and in details of the dome.

Between the Warrant Design and the final one, lay the Penultimate. In this the curious spire was replaced by a dome on a drum pierced by sixteen oval windows between consoles, but the dome was not dominant enough, being only about two hundred feet in height, which was one hundred feet less than that of the Great Model. Wren therefore added screen walls adorned with double orders, as on Jones's Banqueting Hall, above the aisle walls to make the body of the building voluminous enough to carry a much larger and loftier dome placed on a great drum, as well as to serve as weights to counter the outward thrust of the dome on hidden flying buttresses.

While Wren was modifying his design, the old building was being demolished. This was no easy task for the walls were eighty feet high and five feet thick; moreover, the mortar was exceptionally hard, suggesting the existence of a London building tradition going back to the Roman occupation. The task was not made any easier by the large quantities of roof lead which had congealed on the walls. The lead was recovered for recasting, some of the stones of the old structure were set aside for re-use, and rubble was laid in heaps and later removed for street-laying. Pickaxes were employed of course, but the tower was partly demolished with the help of gunpowder until a second blast shot a stone into the room of a private house where some women were sitting at work; luckily no harm was done but no more powder was thereafter used. Finally a battering ram worked by thirty men was applied to the loftier walls, and after long persistence toppled the stonework. About a hundred and twenty-four labourers were employed on the demolition of Old St Paul's.

New foundations were then laid which missed the old ones, the one trouble being at the north-east corner where an ancient pit of potters' earth filled with sherds was discovered so that a ditch had to be dug through it forty feet down to a level containing water and sea shells where a solid raft of masonry was laid.

Wren had hoped to surround his cathedral, as now outlined by the foundations, with wide spaces, particularly at the western approach, hoping thus to emulate Bernini's arcades and grand piazza of St Peter's, Rome, but the cost of acquiring sufficient land proved to be prohibitive. Today, after the local re-building and replanning accomplished since the last war, the cathedral has more space around it than it previously enjoyed, and it can be seen as a whole

72. *Canaletto's painting of St Paul's Cathedral.*

73. *The west front of one of Wren's abortive schemes for the Cathedral with its curious pagoda-like spire and its portico in the manner of Inigo Jones. Having been approved by the king it was called the Warrant Design.*

from a distance; at the same time the pristine and grandiloquent scale has been degraded by the surrounding office towers, by an ill-mannered projection towards the top of Ludgate Hill, and by the inept attachments of the choir school on the east.

During the thirty-five years of building Wren was continually on the site, making a regular tour of inspection every Saturday. Ten years after the first stone was laid in 1675, the walls of the choir and the aisles were up and the great piers of the dome were at the same height. By 1700 the drum of the upper dome and the bases of the western towers were complete and in 1708 the younger Christopher Wren laid the last stone on the top of the lantern. The building was virtually finished and that year Wren attended his last meeting of the commissioners. In 1711 Parliament officially declared the grand edifice open. 'Thus', declares *Parentalia* proudly, 'was this mighty fabric, the second church for grandeur in Europe, in the space of 35 years, begun and finished by one architect, and under one Bishop of London, Dr Henry Compton . . . whereas the Church of St Peter in Rome (the only edifice that can come in competition with it) continued in the building space of 145 years, carried on by no less than twelve architects successively; assisted by the police and the interests of the Roman-See; the ready acquisition of marble, and attended by the best artists of the world . . . during the reigns of nineteen Popes.'

Parentalia also records an incident that occurred during the initial stages of building which seemed to many to be a memorable omen. Wren had set out on the site the dimensions of the great dome and to fix the centre had ordered a workman to bring him a flat stone from one of the heaps of rubble that

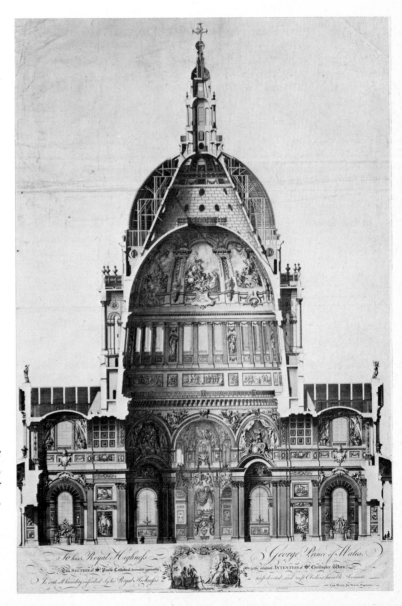

74. *An engraving of 1755 of the section of the double dome, supporting brick cone and interior decorations of Wren's final design.*

would serve as a marker for the masons. The stone brought back happened to be a piece of gravestone bearing the single word in large capitals: RESURGAM (I rise again).

More than fifty thousand tons of Portland stone were needed for the cathedral, as well as twenty-five thousand tons of other kinds of stone from Reigate, Headington and Ketton, also five hundred tons of rubble, eleven thousand tons of ragstone, to say nothing of wagon-loads of marble, bricks, timber, copper, lead and iron. The total cost was about three-quarters of a million pounds.

The way the structure of the cathedral works is not obvious at first sight and takes some understanding; the design is in several ways ambiguous. We have already seen how the walls of choir and nave were built. The dome is even more complex; there are, in fact, two domes – one for internal effect and another above it standing on a drum for high external effect to form as impressive a landmark as the tower and spire of Old St Paul's had been. Between the two domes rises a brick cone supporting the stone lantern and the copper-gilt ornaments above it, but hidden by the outer dome of lead-covered timber. Seen from within, the outer dome, if exposed, would have formed a void far too high and cavernous to please the eye. Between the upper dome and the cone are easy stairs ascending to the lantern with its circular balcony.

The inner dome is pierced at its centre with an eye like that of the Pantheon in Rome, and is otherwise covered with paintings and decorations in eight compartments depicting the history of St Paul. Sir James Thornhill, who also painted the ceiling of the Great Hall at Greenwich, was commissioned to do the work against the wishes of Wren, who not only wanted the inner dome to be decorated with magnificent mosaics in the Italian manner like those of St Peter's, but found the paintings absurdly unrelated to the architectural forms they covered.

Although the dome would no doubt have stood on its own, for greater caution Wren held its thrust in with a double chain of iron embedded in lead inside a channel encircling the base of the dome. The whole is supported on eight enormous piers faced with twin pilasters carrying eight arches, the octagon thus formed being transferred to the circle of the dome by intermediate pendentives. At the diagonals, lower segmental arches span bays leading into the aisles which give a somewhat clumsy effect, as also do the caverns below the main diagonal arches which are darkened by the external screen walls hiding the flying buttresses. In spite of this lack of structural clarity, the great domed space, unprecedented in England, retains its magnificence.

On the west front, the double orders of superimposed and coupled columns reduce the grandeur of scale which a single row of giant columns would have

75. *St Paul's from the south-west as seen by Malton in 1790.*

provided. It is a typical example of adaptive Wren compromise, being enforced, as we have noticed, by the limited sizes of Portland stone blocks. Yet the double range of columns does provide a link with the double orders on the north and south walls. The exterior as a whole is dignified and impressive, not least on account of the strong geometrical modelling, particularly of the carved porches at the east end and at the ends of the transept that harmonize formally so well with the curves of the dome and its drum. The immense size and complexity of the structure, even in this modern age of advanced techniques, remains breathtaking in its serene solidity, however often it is seen.

Wren decided to ignore the terms of the Warrant which directed the completion of the building in piecemeal parts starting with the choir, because he feared that if one part were finished, interest in the whole would wane. So the work proceeded in all parts under a number of master masons, each of whom was responsible for a part, among them Thomas Strong, foreman of the whole works (soon superseded by his younger brother Edward), Samuel Fulkes and Christopher Kempster, builder of Abingdon Town Hall. The admirable Strongs, who between them saw the start and the finish of the great work, belonged to a family of Oxfordshire quarry owners, and may have come to London after the Fire when the guild ban on provincial craftsmen was lifted. Edward Strong, who by 1694 had no less than sixty-five skilled masons assisting him, became a wealthy man; his bones lie below a splendid marble monument in St Peter's Church, St Albans.

With the rebuilding of the City in general and of the cathedral in particular, a fine English school of craftsmanship, begun in the days of Inigo Jones, achieved maturity; it continued up to the Industrial Revolution and beyond. At St Paul's only the best men were employed. The most important carver there, both in stone and in wood, was Grinling Gibbons who was born at Rotterdam, presumably of English parents. He was seen at work through a cottage window in 1670 by John Evelyn who realized he was watching a genius and acted accordingly to promote his discovery. Gibbons, indeed, has since been named the most famous craftsman in English history. Some of his stone carvings, such as festoons, can be seen on the outer walls of the cathedral but his most exquisite work is in the high-reliefs of the woodwork of stalls, organ case, and bishop's throne. Mostly he favoured deeply cut flowers, foliage, ribbons and putti, partly inspired by Dutch floral paintings.

Jonathan Maine and William Kempster also executed some excellent carving at St Paul's, and so did the Dane, Caius Gabriel Cibber, notably the keystones of the arches below the dome and the emblematic phoenix above the south portico. When Cibber died in 1700, Francis Bird took his place and was responsible, among other things, for the large group in marble in the west pediment depicting the conversion of St Paul, as well as those important

76. *Malton's grand view of the Nave of St Paul's c. 1790.*

figures silhouetted against the sky along the tops of the outer walls and the statue of Queen Anne that stands in front of the cathedral – all skilful work though pedestrian. Another valuable craftsman was the ornamental iron-worker, Jean Tijou, a Huguenot refugee, who made most of the magnificent gates and grilles inside the cathedral as well as the simple stair rails and window screens.

The Victorians took a dislike to Renaissance architecture; the medievalist Pugin, who designed the details of Barry's Houses of Parliament, called the dome of St Paul's 'fictitious' and 'a more imposing show, constructed at a vast expense without any legitimate reason', while Ruskin objected to the double dome and screen walls. In Edwardian days enthusiasm for Wren's work

77. *The Choir of St Paul's in 1706.*

returned. The interior was altered in some ways during Victoria's reign. Stained glass was inserted in the windows (removed after the war) and the mosaic decorations were added to the roof of the choir and the spandrels beneath the dome. The screen and organ were moved, destroying Wren's sense of enclosure of choir and crossing, and so were the choir stalls, while the floor of the choir was raised. The worst Victorian addition, however, was a reredos of pink marble which, happily, has gone.

The last years of the building of St Paul's, when the architect could hope to see his greatest work completed and admired, were marred by difficulties and indignities. In order to speed the work, Parliament with unbelievable meanness had suspended half of Wren's modest salary from 1697 until the completion in 1711 when the arrears, after some fuss, were paid. The delays were by no means all Wren's fault; for one thing, stone deliveries were held up after a serious landslide at the Portland quarries. There was also some jobbery when the contract for the railings around the cathedral area was given, over Wren's head, to a squalid character called Jones – after which episode Wren refused to attend another meeting of the Commission. He was also snubbed when Thornhill was commissioned to execute the paintings on the dome against his wishes, and then the tops of the cathedral walls were completed with an open balustrade instead of Wren's design for a solid parapet. On this his cool comment was that 'ladies think nothing well without an edging'.

78. *Grinling Gibbons, the great carver, painted c. 1690.*

Wren sadly outlived the age to which he belonged; he was no longer popular as the new Palladianism gained fashion. Finally, in 1718 at the age of eighty-six, as a result of further jobbery, Wren was dismissed from his post as Surveyor-General, under the accusations of mismanagement, though he was allowed to retain the title. Sir John Vanbrugh might have succeeded him as Surveyor-General but declined the offer 'out of tenderness to Sir Christopher Wren'. An incompetent nonentity named William Benson was given the job, but he did not hold it for long. This was an unmerited end to a long career of tireless and creative dedication through no less than five reigns. In a dignified acceptance he wrote to the commissioners that he had 'endeavoured to do his Majesty all the service I was able, with the same integrity and zeal which I had ever practised'. He suggested that the commissioners, and not he, should be asked to answer the charges of mismanagement, and concluded 'as I am dismissed, having worn out (by God's mercy) a long life in the royal service, and having made some figure in the world, I hope it will be allowed me to die in peace'.

Although he remained Surveyor of Westminster Abbey till his death, Wren went into retirement at Hampton Court, 'in which recess,' states *Parentalia*, 'free from worldly affairs, he passed the greatest part of the five following years of his life in contemplation and studies, and principally in the consolation of the holy Scriptures; chearful in solitude, and as well pleased to die in the shade as in the light.'

8. Final View

Wren caught a cold and died during an afternoon nap on 25 February 1723 at his town house in St James's Street at the age of ninety-one. 'His great humanity appeared to the last, in benevolence and complacency, free from all moroseness in behaviour and aspect', wrote his son. The following week he was borne to his cathedral 'with great funeral state and solemnity' and was there buried in the crypt.

How did the restored City, to which Wren had contributed so much, look at the time of his death?

The differences from the old medieval city were striking. Although the old street lay-out had been retained, if improved by widening and reduction of gradients to ease the flow of traffic, particularly from west to east, the fabric and appearance of buildings was quite fresh; indeed they were revolutionary. All timber-framed buildings had gone and the new City was one of brick and

79. *An ivory relief of Sir Christopher Wren in old age.*

stone applied under high standards and displaying a new and urbane homo-
geneity in the street façades. All the slummy, insanitary confusion of hovels had
gone and with it the old risks of fire and pestilence.

'No one of the improvements can be described as spectacular', writes Reddaway. 'London had become a citizen's city, and had none of the absolute monarch's
inclination towards the grandiose . . . The changes were far-reaching but
utilitarian. The rebuilt area had its splendour, but it was the sober splendour of
the Dutch towns – exemplars of burgherdom – of row upon row of seemly,
well-built brick houses . . . The parish churches, its finest adornment, owed their
beauty almost to an accident. No effort was made to site them to greater advantage . . . Monuments of pious conservatism, they might well have been dull
or mediocre. Only the chance genius of one man raised them to a splendour
undreamt of by their parishioners. St Paul's Cathedral was the only building
that could challenge Europe.'

In a letter to Wren, Dr Woodward, lecturer at Gresham College, con-
gratulated the architect on his part of the rebuilding and then summed up the
general improvements: 'The Fire however disastrous it might be to the then
inhabitants, had proved infinitely beneficial to their posterity; conducing
vastly to the improvement and the increase, as well of the riches and opulence,
as of the splendour of this city. Then, which I and every body must observe,
with great satisfaction, by means of the inlargements of the streets; of the great
plenty of good water, conveyed to all parts; of the common sewers, and other
like contrivances, such provision is made for a free access and passage of the air,
for sweetness, for cleanness, and for salubrity, that is not only the finest, but
the most healthy city in the World.'

The new City was the result, partly of the fortuitous presence of a single
outstanding architect, but partly also of the two exceptionally intelligent
Rebuilding Acts that produced the general improvements as well as the coherent
domestic vernacular. As with the by-pass villas and housing estates of our own
times, no names of architects are identified with any of the nine thousand new
houses of the rebuilt City with their red brickwork, tiled roofs, carved eaves
and doorways, tall, rhythmical casement windows, general fire-proof solidity,
elegant proportions and balustraded staircases within, all set to form continuous,
dignified street façades. As contemporary prints and paintings show, the general
scene that had replaced the country-town look of the old City was appropriate
to a great capital.

The City had risen again in a new form. Its appearance from the river was as
different from the medieval, pre-Fire picture as from that we see today. With
its tiled roofs pierced by the variegated steeples surmounted by glinting weather
vanes of the fifty-one churches, mostly of Portland stone and largely the pro-
ducts of Wren's fertile fantasy, it possessed a charm, immutability, and unity

80. *An eighteenth-century painting of the riverside showing the old bridge from the west still bearing its houses. Fishmongers' Hall is on the left with the Fire Monument behind it where the Fire began.*

of scale that have long since vanished. The whole picture, held together by the great dome on its drum, swelling, matriarchal, and gleaming white as a wedding-cake against the blues and greys of the English sky, appeared from the river as one of the most comely in Europe, a complete new town pleasing enough in its looks to inspire Canaletto's most memorable townscapes. All the colouring was new – the warm reds of the tiles and the russets of the brick-work, enlivened by white-painted trim, to which the informal patches of living, leafy green, the occasional low, grey rectangles of the leaded church roofs, and the graceful ivory steeples thrusting joyfully through them provided vigorous foils. The gay freshness of it all was its most striking trait, an elegant freshness, for the age of cultivated taste had arrived and with it a pride in fine craftsmanship.

Among the vertical features was the Monument, the tall fluted Doric column of Portland stone that commemorated the Great Fire and the rebuilding of the City, which can still be seen and climbed near the spot where the Fire broke out close to the northern head of London Bridge. Begun in 1671 but not completed until 1677, it offered an opportunity to the designers to emulate a Roman type of structure. 'It much exceeds in height the pillars of Rome', states *Parentalia*. 'In the place of the brass-urn on the top (which is not artfully performed, and was set up contrary to his [Wren's] opinion) was originally intended a coloss statue in brass gilt, of King Charles the Second, as founder of the new City; in the manner of the Roman pillars, which terminated with the statues of their

Caesars; or else, a figure erect of a woman crowned with turrets, holding a sword, and cap of maintenance, with other ensigns of the City's grandeur, and re-erection. The altitude, from the pavement, is 202 feet; the ground bounded by the plinth or lowest part of the pedestal is 28 feet square; and the pedestal in height is 40 feet. Within, is a large stair-case of black marble, containing 345 steps . . . Over the capital is an iron balcony encompassing a cippus, or meta, 32 feet high, supporting a blazing urn of brass gilt. Prior to this, the surveyor (as it appears by an original drawing) had made a design of a pillar . . . after a peculiar device; for, as the Romans expressed by relievo, on the pedestals, and round the shafts of their columns, the history of such actions and incidents as were intended to be thereby commemorated; so this Monument of the conflagration, and resurrection of the City of London, was represented by a pillar of flames; the flames, blazing from the loopholes of the shaft (which were to give light to the stairs within), were figured in brass-work gilt; and on the top was a phoenix rising from her ashes, of brass gilt likewise.'

This would have been a more exciting design than the one we know, whose high vase blazes tamely, the whole appearing, according to Defoe, like a candle. Wren discarded this phoenix design on account not only of cost but also because he thought it might be dangerous 'by reason of the sail the spread wings will carry in the winde'.

The position of the Monument is also tame for it stands in a dip at a low level and is now enveloped by tall buildings of a much later date. Originally it stood on the axis of the old bridge with a certain monumental effect, but it no longer does so since the new bridges were built slightly further to the west.

The emblematic bas-relief on the west side of the square plinth is by Cibber, the Dane who was favoured by Wren and received the appointment of Carver to the King's Closet. It shows the King in a toga giving protection to the ruined city and freedom to its rebuilders and inhabitants. The City is personified by a languishing lady who is being lifted up by Time, winged but balding. Two goddesses above are seated on a cloud, one holding a cornucopia denoting Plenty, the other with a palm branch denoting Peace. There is a bee-hive representing Industry, there are burning houses, citizens gesticulating, a supporting dragon, a royal attendant representing Science, another Architecture, and a third Liberty, who is waving a hat. The king's brother, the Duke of York, is there with sword in hand; also Justice crowned, Fortitude taking a lion for a walk, some energetic labourers at work, and under the king's feet the figure of Envy with pendulant breasts belching fumes. And so on in endless edification. The other three sides of the pedestal are covered with Latin inscriptions which are no doubt also edifying to the few who can understand what they mean.

An inscription was placed on the Monument in 1681 by order of the Court

of Aldermen, who had Titus Oates in mind, but it is no longer there. It read:
'This pillar was set up in perpetual remembrance of that most dreadful burning
of this Protestant city, begun and carried on by ye treachery and malice of ye
Popish faction in ye year of our Lord 1665, in order for carrying on their horrid
plott for extirpating the Protestant and old English liberty, and introducing
Popery and slavery.' In 1685, under James II, this was obliterated, but in 1689
under William III it was reinstated. Pope was to comment:

> *Where London's column, pointing to the skies,*
> *Like a tall bully, lifts its head and lies.*

The inscription was again removed in 1830.

Finally, how are we to assess Wren as a human being and as an architect?
His personality is elusive for although his contemporaries, with very few exceptions, loved and admired him, they say little about him – even the garrulous
Aubrey. Evelyn called him 'that incomparable genius'; Pepys spoke of him
with affection; both knew him well as members of the Royal Society. In spite
of the jealousies success always engenders, none questioned his immense
capabilities. A Frenchman who met him in London described him as 'a slight
little man, but at the same time one of the most civil and frank that I have met
in England'. With the single exception of William Talman he always worked
harmoniously with his colleagues and encouraged his subordinates. Small and

81. *An engraving of the City seen from the south bank in the eighteenth century.*

neat in appearance, he seems to have been of a temperate nature, courteous, unaffected, imperturbable, somewhat aloof. His probing intelligence was prodigious, and conditioned as he was by his education and inclination towards mathematical and scientific ratiocination, his creative emotions tended to be trammelled by his intellect. His works are calmer and lack the baroque passion and theatricality of his less prolific contemporaries such as Vanbrugh, Hawksmoor and Archer. He was clearly very ambitious and a good man of business.

'Further 'tis observable', eulogized his son, 'that he was happily endued with such an evenness of temper, a steady tranquillity of mind, and christian fortitude, that no injurious incidents, or inquietudes of human life, could ever ruffle or discompose; and was in practice a stoick . . . As was said on another occasion by an elegant writer "His knowledge had a right influence on the temper of his mind, which had all the humility, graceful modesty, goodness, calmness, strength, and sincerity of a sound and unaffected philosopher . . ."'

That Wren could sometimes display a spirited anger, in spite of his 'steady tranquillity of mind' appears to be shown in one of John Aubrey's anecdotes: 'It ought never to be forgot, what our ingenious countryman Sir Christopher Wren proposed to the silk-stocking-weavers of London, viz. a way to weave seven pair or nine pair of stockings at once (it must be an odd number). He demanded four hundred pounds for his invention: but the weavers refused it, because they were poor: and besides, they said it would spoil their trade; perhaps they did not consider the proverb, that light gains, with quick returns, make heavy purses. Sir Christopher was so noble, seeing they would not venture so such money, he breaks the model of the engine all to pieces, before their faces.' Was Wren annoyed, or was he really displaying nobility by destroying his model because it might 'spoil their trade'?

Apart from the death mask of All Souls College, the best likeness we have of Wren is the bust by one of his finest craftsmen, the mason and sculptor Edward Pierce, which was presented to Oxford University by his son Christopher in 1673, the year Wren received the accolade at the age of forty-one; the original can be seen in the Ashmolean Museum, Oxford, but a copy exists at the headquarters of the Royal Institute of British Architects in London. The bust, which is a fine one, reveals beneath the large, curly wig, a calm, dignified, patient, sensitive but far from humourless face with a prominent nose and lively, widely set eyes beneath a high forehead. The mouth is generous and mobile, as if he was about to speak. A strong face, slightly Voltairian, though neither cynical nor bitter.

Few architects in history have rivalled the extent, variety and skill of Wren's creations. In spite of his frailty, his energy and application were as astonishing as his ability to cope with difficulties and frustrations. He was, of course, lucky in being presented with exceptional opportunities; on the other hand he was handicapped by lack of study abroad, apart from his visit to Paris, and by lack also of that discussion and rivalry with peers that stimulated his continental contemporaries. And he had to do his best with limited funds, an important fact of life that rarely bothered those patronized abroad by Louis XIV and the Church of Rome. He made mistakes, he compromised, but he got the work done with the minimum of fuss – work that displays at its best remarkable ingenuity, variety, decorum and strength.

Geometry was the basis not only of his structural techniques but of his aesthetic approach. The crown of his achievement, the splendid dome and drum of St Paul's alone, gives evidence of that. The puritan faith in mere functionalism, which still bedevils so much modern design, is not applicable to Wren's works; true functionalism is more than unfeeling utilitarianism, and to understand the architecture of the age of Wren – indeed that of any age – one must

82. *Canaletto's well-known panorama from the terrace of Somerset House in the Strand reveals the post-Fire City skyline about 1740 when the Cathedral and all Wren's churches had been built.*

83. *The medal struck in 1723 to commemorate the death of Sir Christopher Wren.*

attempt to understand the whole period and the context in which it was con-
ceived and not judge it solely from our own view. In a tract, Wren declared of
the three principles of Vitruvius, that beauty and firmness 'depend upon geometrical reasons of optics and statics; the third only (convenience) makes the
variety'. Since 'architecture aims at eternity' it must be based on the classical
orders, that are 'uncapable of modes and fashions'. A function of architecture,
he states, is political, 'public buildings being the ornament of a country; it
establishes a nation, draws people and commerce; makes the people love their
native country, which passion is the original of all great actions in a commonwealth.'

In another tract, Wren supports the approach of genuine functionalism:
'It seems very unaccountable, that the generality of our late architects dwell
so much upon this ornamental, and so slightly pass over the geometrical,
which is the most essential part of architecture . . . For instance, can an *arch*
stand without butment sufficient? . . . Geometrical figures are naturally more
beautiful than other irregular; in this all consent as to a Law of Nature.'

However ideas on Laws of Nature or fashions in design may change,
Wren's monumental place not only in London's history but in that of the whole
of Britain will remain unassailable. He was a man of rare qualities whose
influence changed the fabric of the country. To the question, 'Who is England's
greatest architect', can any other answer yet be given than Christopher Wren?

THE MONUMENT

This Pillar was set up in perpetual remembrance of y most
dreadfull Burning of this City,
Anno 1666, on three sides of the
Pedestal are Inscriptions which
give an account thereof, on
the other there are proper
Hierogly phick figures carved in Relievo, and at Top
there is Golden Flames proceeding out of an urn, the
Monument stands on a large
Vault of Stone Arched over,
the Pedestal is 21 foot and 6
square and 27 foot high, the

the Column is of the Dorick
Order and measures 47 foote
& in Circumference, its Diameter
from out to out is 15 foot, and
9 foot within, its height from
the Pedestal to the Balcone
is 133 foot, and from the Balcony to the top of y Flames
is thirty eight foot. So that
the height of the Monument
from the ground is 202 foot,
the whole of it is a curious
piece of Workmanship and
cost upwards of 13700 Pounds
in Building.

Fish Street Hill

84. *The Monument erected near the spot where the Fire broke out. It was built on the axis of the
approach to old London Bridge before Rennie's bridge was completed slightly further west in 1831.*

Notes on the Illustrations

The publishers would like to thank the owners of the pictures listed below for their permission to reproduce them in this edition.

1. The Great Fire of London. The view is looking up river from Wapping. On the right is the Tower of London, on the left London Bridge with its houses and in the distance Old St Paul's in full blaze. Contemporary oil painting by an unknown artist. *The Worshipful Company of Goldsmiths*.

2. The Choir of St Paul's Cathedral in Wren's rebuilding. The superb detailing, including the wood carving by Grinling Gibbons and the iron-work by Tijou, can here be clearly seen. Wren placed the great carved organ at the west end of the Choir and a screen at the other in order to create a sense of enclosure. Oil painting by an unknown artist. *The Worshipful Company of Goldsmiths*.

3. View of London, 1616. Part of Vischer's famous engraved panorama showing the chaotic charm of London seen from a distance with its forest of medieval spires. St Saviour's Church which became Southwark Cathedral is on the bottom right by the Bridge. *Maré Collection*.

4. Typical pre-Fire London houses, as shown in an engraving in the *Maré Collection*.

5. Map of Elizabethan London in 1572. Hand-coloured engraving by Frans Hogenberg. In the left-hand top corner are the arms of Elizabeth and in the right-hand corner those of the City. The original is nineteen inches wide and was published in Braun and Hogenburg's *Civitates Orbis Terrarum*. *London Museum*.

6. Prospect of the Nave of Old St Paul's Cathedral, 1658. Engraving by Wenceslaus Hollar (1607–77). Hollar came from Prague and was patronized by the Earl of Arundel, who brought him to London where he produced many topographical etchings both before and after the Fire. *London Museum*.

7. Buildings in Westcheap at the west end of Cheapside, London's main market with the old church of St Michael in the Querne. The Little Conduit is at the centre surrounded by water jugs. Drawing by Ralph Treswell, 1585. *British Museum*.

8. Covent Garden with its piazzas surrounding a green and St Paul's parish church. Designed by Inigo Jones for the Duke of Bedford as the first of London's famous west-end squares built as specula-

tions by aristocratic Londoners. *British Museum*.

9. James I and his family listening to a sermon at St Paul's Cross. Part of the painting known as 'Farley's Dream' painted by Gypkin in 1616 and commissioned by Farley, who wanted the old cathedral – by then very dilapidated – restored to its former state. After much persuasion by Farley, who wrote a book in verse describing his vision, the king agreed to the restoration and he and his family came to St Paul's in 1620 to hear a sermon. The painting, by then four years old, has been taken as a representation of this event, but is not in fact so. *Society of Antiquaries*.

10. Charles II's entry into the City at the Restoration in 1660. Contemporary engraving. *British Museum*.

11. Inigo Jones (1573–1651). His most famous surviving building which influenced Wren is the Banqueting Hall in Whitehall. Oil painting after Vandyck. *National Portrait Gallery*.

12. The Lord Mayor's annual water procession on the Thames which took to the land in 1856 to become the Lord Mayor's Show. Oil painting by an unknown artist. *Property of Her Majesty the Queen*.

13. Fleeing from the Plague. An engraving as a broadsheet entitled 'London Sounds a Trumpet that the Countrey may heare it'. *Society of Antiquaries*.

14. Old St Paul's Cathedral, east elevation, 1658. Engraving by Wenceslaus Hollar. *Department of the Environment*.

15. Old St Paul's Cathedral, 1658, showing original steeple before lightning damage. The south portico is one of the Italianate changes wrought by Inigo Jones. Engraving by Wenceslaus Hollar. *Department of the Environment*.

16. Coronation Procession of Edward VI through the City. Wall painting – a copy of the original once at Cowdray Hall, Sussex, by an unknown artist. *Society of Antiquaries*.

17. The old Royal Exchange, built in 1568, in classical style, destroyed in the Fire. Engraving by Wenceslaus Hollar. *London Museum*.

18. Portrait of Sir Christopher Wren. Oil painting by Antonio Verrio, Sir Godfrey Kneller and Sir James Thornhill. *Sheldonian Theatre, Oxford*.

85. *A miniature watercolour sketch of St Paul's, from the mouth of the Fleet Canal, painted by Malton.*

19. Wren's pre-Fire design for a new dome over the crossing of Old St Paul's Cathedral. Wren's own original drawing. *All Souls College, Oxford.*

20. Section of Wren's proposed dome over the crossing of Old St Paul's. Wren's own drawing. *All Souls College, Oxford.*

21. Charles II. Oil painting by J. M. Wright (detail). *Property of Her Majesty the Queen.*

22. Coat of Arms of Sir Christopher Wren. Oil painting by an unknown artist. *Royal Hospital, Chelsea.*

23. Christopher Wren, son of Sir Christopher Wren. Oil painting by an unknown artist. *Department of the Environment.*

24. Fire of London Medal, 1666. *British Museum.*

25. Samuel Pepys (1633–1703), in 1666. Oil painting by J. Hayls. *National Portrait Gallery.*

26. Title page of a sermon preached before the king on 10 October 1666, by William Sandcroft, Dean of St Paul's with an engraving of Old St Paul's Cathedral on fire, by an unknown artist. *London Library.*

27. A fire engine designed by John Keeling of Black Fryers. Engraving by an unknown artist. *Mary Evans Picture Library.*

28. The Great Fire of London. On the left is Ludgate and in the distance Old St Paul's with the tower of St Mary-le-Bow to its right. Oil painting after Jan Griffier the elder. *London Museum.*

29. John Evelyn (1620–1706). Engraving by Thomas Worlidge, 1723. *Mary Evans Picture Library.*

30. The Great Fire of London, looking up river from Wapping. Oil painting, Dutch School. *London Museum.*

31. John Lofting's fire engine. Engraving by J. Kip. *Society of Antiquaries.*

32. King Charles II, walking with his courtiers on Horse Guards Parade, *c.* 1680. In the distance can be seen the Banqueting Hall of Inigo Jones. Oil painting by Tillimans. *Property of the Duke of Roxburghe.*

33. James II, as Duke of York, *c.* 1660. Diamond etching on glass. *Property of Denys E. Bower, Esq.*

34. A silver mug commemorating the Great Fire of London with a Latin inscription. *London Museum.*

35. London's dreadful visitation. Title page of a collection of the Bills of Mortality for the year beginning 27 December 1664. *Magdalene College, Cambridge.*

36. Gresham House and College. Engraving by George Vertue, 1739. *British Museum.*

37. Arundel House. Etching by Wenceslaus Hollar, 1646. *British Museum.*

38. The frozen Thames. Oil painting by Abraham Hondius, 1677. *London Museum.*

39. Wax effigy of Charles II in the crypt of Westminster Abbey.

40. Wren's plan for rebuilding the City after the Fire. Contemporary engraving. *Maré Collection.*

41. Ruins of Old St Paul's showing the west portico designed by Inigo Jones. Drawing by T. Wyck. *Bodleian Library, Oxford.*

42. Charles II. Oil painting by an unknown artist. *National Portrait Gallery.*

43. Sir John Evelyn's plan for rebuilding the City. Engraving by an unknown artist. *Maré Collection.*

44. The Thames and the entrance to the Fleet Canal at Blackfriars. Oil painting probably by Samuel Scott. The spire of St Bride's is on the left and that of St Martin Ludgate on the right, both by Wren. *Property of Her Majesty the Queen.*

45. Sir Matthew Hale, President of the Fire Court, *c.* 1670. Oil painting by J. M. Wright. *National Portrait Gallery.*

46. A London coffee house, *c.* 1700. Watercolour by an unknown artist. *British Museum.*

47. A view from the west end of the Custom House Quay. Oil painting *c.* 1700 by William Marlow. *Guildhall Art Gallery.*

48. Fishmongers' Hall. Engraving by Sutton Nicholls. *British Museum.*

49. Wren's Custom House of brick with stone dressings. It was burned down in 1718. Engraving by an unknown artist. *Maré Collection.*

50. The Master, Wardens and Court of Assistants of the Worshipful Company of Joiners and Ceilers receiving the plans for their new Hall, 1694. Oil painting, attributed to Cornelius Janssen. *Worshipful Company of Joiners and Ceilers.*

51. The Royal Exchange of 1671 designed by Edward Jerman. It was burned down in 1838. Engraving by R. White. *London Museum.*

52. Goldsmiths' Hall. A bird's-eye view printed by John Ward, 1691. The original building was designed by Nicholas Stone, but it was gutted by the Fire and Edward Jerman redesigned it. *Worshipful Company of Goldsmiths.*

53. Stone Quarries. Wood engraving by an unknown artist. *Mary Evans Picture Library.*

54. Brick Making. Wood engraving by an unknown artist. *Mary Evans Picture Library.*

55. Mercers' Chapel with adjoining shops and houses as rebuilt after the Fire. Engraving from *London Survey'd* by William Morgan, 1681/2. *British Museum.*

56. Goldsmiths' Hall. Plan by John Ward, 1691. *Worshipful Company of Goldsmiths.*

57. London Rocket, or *Sisymbrium irio* from Jacquin *Florae Austiacae. Royal Botanical Gardens, Kew.*

58. Temple Bar from the west, *c.* 1760. Oil painting by John Collet. *Property of the Earl of Jersey.*

59. Steeple of St Mary-le-Bow. Drawing by Sir Christopher Wren. *Bodleian Library, Oxford.*

60. St Michael Cornhill, west prospect. Engraving by an unknown artist. Gilbert Scott Victorianized this church. *Guildhall Art Gallery.*

61. Interior of St Stephen Walbrook. Aquatint by Thomas Malton, from *Picturesque Tour,* 1792. *Guildhall Art Gallery.*

62. St Magnus Martyr and London Bridge, *c.* 1810. Drawing by Thomas Shepherd. *British Museum.*

63. St Bride's, Fleet Street, 1753. Engraving by Donswell. *Guildhall Art Gallery.*

64. St Lawrence Jewry and the Guildhall. Oil painting by Thomas Malton, *c.* 1790. *Guildhall Art Gallery.*

65. St Mary-le-Bow, Cheapside. Engraving by Bowles. *British Museum.*

66. North front of the Stocks Market in 1738 with Wren's church, St Stephen Walbrook, in the background and a statue of Charles II overcoming Cromwell in the foreground. The Mansion House was built on the site in 1753 and the statue is now at Newby Hall, Ripon. Engraving by Sutton Nichols. *British Museum.*

67. St Stephen Walbrook, 1811. Drawing by Thomas Shepherd. *British Museum.*

68. Plan of the Great Model. *Sir John Soane's Museum.*

69. The Great Model. *The Dean and Chapter of St Paul's Cathedral.*

70. St Paul's Cathedral. Ground Plan 1726. Engraving by an unknown artist. *Guildhall Art Gallery.*

71. The Thames at Horseferry, *c.* 1700. The dome of St Paul's is inaccurately painted as the picture was finished before the scaffolding was removed. Oil painting. English School. *London Museum.*

72. St Paul's with figures, 1740. Oil painting by Antonio Canaletto. *Collection of Mr and Mrs Paul Mellon.*

73. The Warrant Design, west front. Contemporary drawing by an unknown artist. *All Souls College, Oxford.*

74. Section of St Paul's Cathedral showing the interior decoration in an engraving of 1755 by an unknown artist. *Guildhall Art Gallery.*

75. South-west view of St Paul's, 1790. Aquatint by Thomas Malton. Wren's church of St Augustine-with-St Faith is in the distance. Only the tower of the church now remains. *British Museum.*

76. Nave of St Paul's from the west, *c.* 1790. Aquatint by Thomas Malton. *Guildhall Art Gallery.*

77. The Choir of St Paul's, 1706. Engraving by Robert Trevitt. *British Museum.*

78. Grinling Gibbons (1648–1721), *c.* 1690. Oil painting after Kneller. *National Portrait Gallery.*

79. Sir Christopher Wren, *c.* 1723. Ivory oval by David Le Marchand. *National Portrait Gallery.*

80. The Thames at London Bridge. The old bridge still retains its houses, now in decay and removed in the early 1760s. Oil painting, school of Samuel Scott. *Property of Her Majesty the Queen.*

81. A view of the City. Early eighteenth-century engraving by an unknown artist. *British Museum.*

82. View of the Thames from Somerset House, *c.* 1740. Oil painting by Antonio Canaletto. *Property of Her Majesty the Queen.*

83. Sir Christopher Wren Medal, 1723, commemorating his death. *British Museum.*

84. The Monument. Engraving by Sutton Nicholls. *Guildhall Art Gallery.*

85. Watercolour sketch of St Paul's, *c.* 1790, by Thomas Malton. *The Folio Society.*

A PROSPECT of the CITY of LONDON from S.ᵗ MARIE

Cathedral of S.ᵗ Paul

THE RIVER TH

Another PROSPECT of the above CITY taken from the Same

DATE DUE

OC 26 '81			
NOV 6 '86			
SEP 29 '88			
FEB 12 '89			
GAYLORD		PRINTED IN U.S.A.

GAYLORD   PRINTED IN U.S.A.

A Plan fo... Design'd by that
but unhappily Defe

REFERENCE to the

1 S. Benet	25 S. Ba
2 S. Andrew in Wardrop	26 S. E
3 S. Peters in Thames street	27 S. M
4 S. Martins by Ludgate	28 Allha
5 S. Andrew in Holborne	29 S. Pe
6 S. Pulchers	30 S. D
7 S. Nicholas	31 S. M
8 S. Christi Church	32 S. A
9 S. Augustines	33 S. M
10 S. Foster	34 B
11 S. John Zachary	35 S. D
12 S. Martins in Thames str.	36 Allha
13 S. Marys Aldermanbury	37 Paul
14 S. Thomas	38 Wat
15 Bow Church	39 S. C
16 S. Laurence	40 Que
17 S. Mary Botolph La.	41 Suli
18 Allhallowes the Gr.	42 Col
19 S. Stephens Colman Str.	43 Old
20 S. Margaret	44 Fil
21 S. Mary Wilnoth	h
22 S. Laurence Poultney	45 di
23 S. Stephens in Walbroke	
24 S. Christopher	

EXPLANATION to

The shadowed part is that which esca

C. Churches   M. Markets

A Scale of 1800 Feet

Charter House Squar

SMITHFIELD

Newgat

Ludgate   Piazze

Wood

M.

Key   Bridewell   Dock   The Grand Terras with the Publick Hal